Toy Poodles as Pets

The Ultimate Toy Poodle's Owner's Guide

Toy Poodle breeding, where to buy, types, care, temperament, cost, health, showing, grooming, diet, and much more included!

By Lolly Brown

Copyrights and Trademarks

Disclaimer and Legal Notice

Foreword

Wherever they are, Toy Poodles stand out – even despite their tiny size. This is the smallest size or variety of Poodle – but the difference is mostly that of height. Altogether, Standard, Miniature and Toy Poodles are still considered as one breed.

The Toy Poodle is known for its high intelligence, affectionate nature, and of course, its amazing, hypoallergenic coat. This can be a high maintenance breed – particularly when it comes to grooming, but the delight and joy they can introduce into your life is well worth the energy investment in maintaining their health and appearance.

The Poodle is the national dog of France, and the breed itself has long been popular among the royal elite in Europe since the 15th century. The Toy Poodle survives today as descendants of those early fashion-working dog pioneers, and their popularity has not waned. Today, they are highly ranked as among the most popular pets among dog owners, and they never fail to capture hearts with their winning personalities and energetic natures.

Table of Contents

Introduction

Toy Poodles are the smallest variety of Poodles – including the Standard and Miniature Poodles. But although these three types are only one breed, kennel clubs such as the AKC recognize these three varieties which are mainly based on their height.

Over the years, the unique cuts and appearance of these dogs have created prejudice of one sort of another in the minds of people – they are dogs for the rich, they don't look like normal dogs, or their haircut makes them look like sissy dogs. Nothing can be farther from the truth.

Of course, caring for a Toy Poodle does require a significant amount of investment in terms of grooming and other expenses – perhaps the main reason why they are mainly pets of the wealthy who can afford their upkeep. But this need not necessarily be true. There are non-show cuts that can make your Poodle less sissy, and their natural temperament will soon convince you that they are anything but. Proper planning and budgeting can help you work your way around the costs – and at the extreme, you might want to teach yourself how to groom your Toy Poodle yourself.

About one thing is certain – Poodle owners will tell you that the cost and all the effort towards maintaining this intelligent and lovable dog is well worth it.

Glossary of Dog Terms

AKC – American Kennel Club, the largest purebred dog registry in the United States

Almond Eye – Referring to an elongated eye shape rather than a rounded shape

Babbler - A hound that gives tongue when not on the trail

Balance – A show term referring to all of the parts of the dog, both moving and standing, which produce a harmonious image

Bay - Prolonged bark of a hunting hound

Beard – Long, thick hair on the dog's underjaw

Best in Show – An award given to the only undefeated dog left standing at the end of judging

Bicolor - A coat of two distinct colors

Bitch – A female dog

Bite – The position of the upper and lower teeth when the dog's jaws are closed; positions include level, undershot, scissors, or overshot

Blaze – A white stripe running down the center of the face between the eyes

Board – To house, feed, and care for a dog for a fee

Break - When the puppy's coat color changes as an adult

Breed – A domestic race of dogs having a common gene pool and characterized appearance/function

Breed Standard – A published document describing the look, movement, and behavior of the perfect specimen of a particular breed

Buff – An off-white to gold coloring

Castrate - The removal of the testicles of a male dog.

Character - The individuality, general appearance, expression and deportment considered typical of a breed.

Clip – A method of trimming the coat in some breeds

Coarse - Lacks refinement.

Coat – The hair covering of a dog; some breeds have two coats, and outer coat and undercoat; also known as a double coat. Examples of breeds with double coats include German Shepherd, Siberian Husky, Akita, etc.

Condition – The health of the dog as shown by its skin, coat, behavior, and general appearance

Conformation - Form and structure of shape and parts in conformance with breed standards

Corky - Lively, active

Crate – A container used to house and transport dogs; also called a cage or kennel

Crossbreed (Hybrid) – A dog having a sire and dam of two different breeds; cannot be registered with the AKC

Cry - Baying or music of hounds

Dam (bitch) – The female parent of a dog;

Dock – To shorten the tail of a dog by surgically removing the end part of the tail.

Dominance - Displays of assertiveness of one dog over other dogs

Double Coat – Having an outer weather-resistant coat and a soft, waterproof coat for warmth; see above.

Drop Ear – An ear in which the tip of the ear folds over and hangs down; not prick or erect

Ear set - A description of where the ears are set on the head

Even bite - Also *level bite,* meeting of upper and lower incisors without any overlapping

Ear leather - The flap of the ear

Feathering – A long fringe of hair on the ears, tail, legs, or body of a dog

Fetch - A game of retrieval

Gait - A pattern of steps with a particular rhythm and footfall

Game - Wild animals being hunted

Genealogy - Also *Pedigree.*

Gestation Period - From the time of mating until birth.

Gun dog - Dog trained to hunt game.

Groom – To brush, trim, comb or otherwise make a dog's coat neat in appearance

Heat - Estrus, fertile period of the female.

Heel – To command a dog to stay close by its owner's side

Hip Dysplasia – A condition characterized by the abnormal formation of the hip joint

Hound - Dogs that hunt game through scent or sight.

Hound-colored - Black, tan and white with a black saddle

Inbreeding – The breeding of two closely related dogs of one breed

Interbreeding - The breeding of dogs of different breeds

Kennel – A building or enclosure where dogs are kept

Lead - Leash

Litter – A group of puppies born at one time

Markings – A contrasting color or pattern on a dog's coat

Mate – To breed a dog and a bitch

Milk teeth - Baby teeth

Mongrel - The result of crossbreeding

Neuter – To castrate a male dog or spay a female dog

Pack - Several hounds kept in one kennel

Pads – The tough, shock-absorbent skin on the bottom of a dog's foot

Parti-Color – A coloration of a dog's coat consisting of two or more definite, well-broken colors; one of the colors must be white

Pedigree – The written record of a dog's genealogy going back three generations or more

Point - A stylized stance of a hunting dog to indicate the location of game

Puppy – A dog under 12 months of age

Purebred – A dog whose sire and dam belong to the same breed and who are of unmixed descent

Retrieve - Bringing back game to the hunter

Saddle - Dark patches over the back

Shedding – The natural process whereby old hair falls off the dog's body as it is replaced by new hair growth.

Sire – The male parent of a dog

Sighthound - Compare with general term Hound: Dogs that hunt by sight

Smooth Coat – Short hair that is close-lying

Spay – The surgery to remove a female dog's ovaries, rendering her incapable of breeding

Stud - Male dog used for breeding

Tricolor - a coat of three distinct colors, usually black, white and tan

Trim – To groom a dog's coat by plucking or clipping

Type - A sum of qualities distinguishing a specific breed or a specific dog

Undercoat – The soft, short coat typically concealed by a longer outer coat

Wean – The process through which puppies transition from subsisting on their mother's milk to eating solid food

Whelping – The act of birthing a litter of puppies

Whiskers - Sensory organs consisting of hairs on the sides of a dog's muzzle

Chapter One: Understanding Toy Poodles

Any Poodle that stands 6 inches or less at the highest point of the shoulders is classified by the AKC as a Toy Poodle. These tiny, intelligent dogs are little furballs of energy – and you might be surprised at just how agile and quick they can be.

This also translates to productive training sessions as their keen intelligence will quickly allow them to learn commands and desired behaviors – making training sessions quite enjoyable for you both. They like having your attention- particularly when it comes to grooming, which is a wonderful way to build and develop your bond as pet and owner.

If you have ever considered getting a Toy Poodle but wasn't sure if this is the right breed for you, read on.

Facts about Toy Poodles

Poodles are an old breed – and nobody really knows where they came from. What we really have are theories on which breeds figured in to their development. What is known that they have been around for a long time – mainly a working retriever breed, in Germany and France. They became particularly popular in France, until they were adopted as the country's national dog. To this day, the expression "French Poodle" creates the association between France and this adorable breed.

The different sizes of Poodles – Standard, Miniature and Toy, appeared soon after. Some say that they smaller versions of the Poodle were mainly just bred down versions of the same breed, but their small size, high intelligence, affectionate nature and dignified and fashionable appearance made them popular pets of the royalty.

The various Poodle clips we see today – the different haircuts that practically identify the Poodle as a breed – were actually developed by those long-ago hunters. Poodles were initially used as water retrievers for game such as ducks, and the smaller versions such as the Toy Poodle were used for sniffing out and locating truffles. The Poodle's haircut was developed to help them swim more efficiently, while still providing them enough insulation from the cold water. This day, however, the various Poodle cuts have become more of a fashion statement than something utilitarian.

This is a high maintenance dog in terms of grooming and in the regular and daily exercise and attention that they need. They are not meant to be left alone for long periods of time, and they also need sufficient mental and physical stimulation on a daily basis to give then an opportunity to direct their boundless energy. To this day, they are one of the most intelligent dogs around, and can very much enrich their owner's lives through their sheer engaging personality and playful nature.

Summary of Toy Poodle Facts

Pedigree: Barbet, Hungarian Water Hound,

AKC Group: Toy Group

Types: In the AKC, the Toy Poodle is one variety of the Poodle Breed, along with Standard and Miniature Poodles. Size in the AKC is determined by height, not by weight.

Breed Size: small

Height: 10 inches (25.4 cm) or under at the highest point of the shoulders

Weight: 6-9 lbs (3-4 kg)

Coat Types: a single layer coat that is either dense and curly, or corded

Coat Texture: ranges from coarse and woolly to soft and wavy

Coat Clips: For conformation shows, acceptable clips in the AKC include the Puppy clip, English Saddle, Continental Clip, or Sporting Clip

Color: Solid colors or parti-colors ranging from blue, gray, silver, brown, apricot, café-au-lait, cream. Patterns include phantom, brindle and sable – but these are considered out of standard by all major registries.

Eyes: Eyes are dark and oval in shape

Ears: Hangs close to the head, with a thickly feathered and long ear leather

Tail: Straight, set high and carried up.

Temperament: Remarkably intelligent, highly responsive and very trainable. Sweet, cheerful, lively and perk, socializes well. Can sometimes be high strung or timid.

Strangers: Toy Poodles do well with people, though not recommended for the roughhousing play of children. They may have a tendency to bark a lot. They make great watchdogs.

Other Dogs: With proper socialization and enough exercise, Toy Poodles do well with other dogs.

Other Pets: With proper socialization and enough exercise, Toy Poodles do well with other pets

Training: Highly intelligent and very trainable

Exercise Needs: Toy Poodles are an active breed that need daily walks and regular play time.

Health Conditions: generally healthy but may be prone to certain health conditions such as Eye Conditions (Progressive Retinal Atrophy (PRA), Cataracts, Glaucoma, Optic Nerve Hypoplasia, and Tear Staining), Luxating Patella, Legg-Calve-Perthes Disease, Intervertebral Disk Disease (IVDD), Epilepsy, Hypoglycemia, Skin Tumors, Tracheal Collapse, Von Willebrand's Disease, Addison's Disease, Cushing's Disease, Gastric Dilatation-Volvulus (Bloat), and Sebaceous Adenitis

Lifespan: average 12-15 years or more

Toy Poodle Breed History

The Toy Poodle is an old breed, dating back for at least 400 years. Nobody really knows where or how the Poodle first began to make its appearance. Some say the Poodle may have originated in Denmark, but the AKC credits Germany, where the Poodle was said to have once been used as a water retrieval dog and referred to as *Pudelhund*. Etymologically, this translates to the German words "Pudel," meaning "one who plays in water" and

"Hund" or dog. It is theorized that the breed itself may have resulted from a cross of the French Barbet and the Hungarian Water Hound.

While it was a popular pet among the royalty from the 15th-16th centuries in countries such as Germany and Spain, it was France, however, who claimed the Poodle as its national breed. It became a very popular breed in France, thus leading to the common parlance "French Poodle." But its actual nomenclature in France is "Caniche," which means "duck dog." Poodles were mainly gun dogs and water retrievers, and their haircut called the "Poodle clip" was developed to help them swim more efficiently in water, while leaving them enough hair on the legs to protect them from extreme cold and sharp reeds.

The larger dogs were eventually bred down to smaller sizes, and these smaller poodle variants became quite popular with royalty, and was considered a stylish companion for trendy ladies. Records date the Toy variety to England as early as the 18th century, and it was said that they were popularly used for truffle hunting, as their tiny feet were less likely to damage the delicate fungi.

Being a very old breed whose popularity has never waned, the Poodles were already a pretty solid breed by the time the UK Kennel Club was founded in 1873. They were actually one of the first dog breeds to be registered. It was officially recognized by the AKC in 1887. Today, there are three official sizes of the Poodle: Standard, Toy, and Miniature.

Chapter Two: Things to Know Before Getting a Toy Poodle

Have you always wanted a Toy Poodle but were unsure whether or not this breed is right for you, your home, and your lifestyle? Are you doubtful about whether or not you can afford to keep a Toy Poodle – given the costs included in their food, vet checkups, and even grooming? In a way, this is a good sign. It means that you care enough about a potential puppy to look at yourself and your capacity to care for them objectively. After all, even if you want a Toy Poodle more than anything, you would certainly be short-changing them if it turns out that you are not really in the best position to care for one.

In this chapter, we look at some of the more pragmatic and practical aspects involved in caring for a Toy Poodle. We also take a closer look at the pros and cons of this breed, to help you determine whether or not this really is the right breed for you.

Do You Need a License?

The laws on dog licenses vary depending on your area or region – some states require licenses, others don't. The only way to be sure is to inquire with your local legislature regarding their most recent laws on dog ownership.

Even if licenses aren't required in your area, there will usually be a provision for voluntary licensing and registration. If this is available, it is highly recommended that you take advantage of it. Not only does this register your dog in your name – your Toy Poodle himself will be identified with the proper tags so that he can be easily identified should he ever get lost. Such dog tags usually include your contact details as those who may have found him attempt to trace him back to you. Make it easy for them to do so by getting a license.

Please remember that licenses are usually issued only after proof of a current vaccine, and are usually coterminous with your dog's vaccine shot, and generally expires at around the same time. In a way, this is also a good way for you to keep track of your dog's rabies vaccinations, and make sure that this is always kept current.

How Many Toy Poodles Should You Keep?

Whether or not you can keep more than one Toy Poodle directly depends on your capacity to care for them. Obviously, two Poodles mean twice the cost in food and equipment, as well as twice the amount of time spent in training, housebreaking, grooming, and medical expenses. And while Toy Poodles don't take up as much room as a larger breed would, two Poodles also mean a larger area set aside for their beds, crates, and play area.

If you feel that this is something you can reasonably do, then by all means go for it. One good thing about keeping more than one pet is that they can keep each other company during those times when you are out of the house. This also ensures continuing socialization skills, as well as the avoidance of needy puppies or dogs developing separation anxiety.

Do Toy Poodles Get Along with Other Pets?

Toy Poodles are notoriously friendly, whether with humans, other dogs, or other pets. For this to happen, however, they must be properly socialized when they are young. Proper behavioral training will also keep them from displaying unwanted behavior such as excessive barking. And as long as you give them enough physical and mental stimulation, their high-strung nature may not even manifest. As long as you give them enough opportunities to expend their excessive energies in productive activities such as exercise, play, or training, they probably won't develop aggressive tendencies, nor would they take it into their heads to bully other pets.

How Much Does it Cost to Keep a Toy Poodle?

In this section, we cover the potential costs of keeping a Toy Poodle. Please remember that the breakdown presented below are only general estimates, and might be higher or lower depending on the prevailing costs of goods and services in your area or region.

Initial Costs

The average purchase price of a Toy Poodle puppy from a reputable breeder can range from a low of $750 to as high as $2,000 or more. Yes, this can be an expensive breed, particularly when you factor in their regular grooming needs. If you adopt a Toy Poodle from a shelter or a rescue, however, you can probably expect to pay around an average of $150-250.

Other initial costs to factor in include:

Spaying or Neutering	$200
Medical Examination	$70
Crate	$95
Training	$110
Leash and Collar	$30
Total	$505

Add in the initial purchase price, registration or licensing fees, food and water bowls, dog toys, and various other supplies and accessories, and look to shelling out upwards of $1,000 on one-time costs for your first year, quite apart from the yearly costs such as food, vaccinations, medical checkups and grooming supplies.

An average breakdown of these yearly costs of owning one Toy Poodle can be seen in the table below:

	In USD	based on conversion rate of 1GBP=1.438 USD	based on conversion rate of 1USD=1.303 AUD
Food expenses	$525	£365.21	684.07AUD
Veterinarian Bills	$699	£486.25	910.79 AUD
Other costs (toys, treats and other accessories)	$545	£379.12	710.13 AUD
Grooming	$700	£486.78	912.10 AUD
Annual Vaccines, Heartworm preventative, and flea preventative	$800	£556.32	1,042.39 AUD
Total	$3,269	£2,273.68	4,259.48 AUD

Again, the above projected costs are only an estimate, but even with this average estimate it is easy to see that caring for a Toy Poodle can cost a bit of money. Some say it is not for the faint of heart. Toy Poodle aficionados will quickly tell you, however, that the cost can be extremely worth it. You have a beautiful canine companion that is loyal, beautiful, dignified, proud, extremely intelligent, and quite capable of carrying away trophies at dog shows. If you are not sure whether or not you can provide well financially for your Toy Poodle, however, then perhaps this is not the right breed for you.

What are the Pros and Cons of Toy Poodles?

To sum things up, below are a general checklist of the pros and cons of the Toy Poodle as a breed. Weigh them carefully, factor in the costs and the attention and care required by this toy breed, before you make your decision.

Pros for Toy Poodles

- Highly intelligent, loyal and affectionate – easy to train
- Hypoallergenic coat – great for those suffering from allergies

- Adaptable and versatile – can live well in a house with a yard or in an apartment
- Good with children, other pets and strangers – provided there is proper socialization, and provided there is no roughhousing games
- Their coat is non-shedding, which means less hair on the carpet or furniture.
- Their intelligence and naturally affectionate nature makes them great therapy, service or seeing eye dogs

Cons for the Toy Poodles

- High maintenance and costly in terms of grooming and maintenance
- An expensive breed that is a bit expensive to care for and maintain
- May be a bit high-strung, has a tendency to bark – makes good watch dogs, but not guard dogs
- Can get bored pretty quickly – needs constant diversion and stimulation
- Requires regular exercise – about twice or thrice a day averaging an hour's worth of walking each day

Chapter Three: Purchasing Your Toy Poodle

Once you have made up your mind that a Toy Poodle is definitely the dog for you, the next thing you will need to look into is where to get one. You have several options: you can purchase from a reputable breeder, or you can adopt from a shelter or rescue. In this chapter, we explore the different avenues by which you might find your Toy Poodle, as well as some tips on selecting a healthy puppy and on how to prepare and puppy-proof your home for the new arrival.

Where Can You Buy Toy Poodles?

It is always a good idea to look for Toy Poodles from a rescue or a shelter first. Not only will this save you money as opposed to purchasing from a breeder, but you will also be opening your home to a dog in need of it.

There are myriad reasons why dogs end up at a shelter – in many cases, they are simply abandoned by their owners when they leave or move to a different place – and yes, sometimes this happens even to the adorable Toy Poodle. You'll probably be surprised at the dogs you will find at rescues – many are even purebreds in good health that may have had the benefit of former training!

Adopting from a Rescue

Adopting a Toy Poodle from a rescue should always be considered first before you consider purchasing a newborn puppy. There are many dog breeds in need of rescue and with no home to go to. Following are lists of rescues in the United States and the UK, which you can explore or use as the starting point for your search.

Wondering where to start? Below is a list of Poodle and Toy Poodle Rescues to get you started:

United States Rescues:

Poodles in Need.
<http://www.poodlesinneed.com/Pages/default.aspx>

Toy Poodle Rescue.
<http://awos.petfinder.com/shelters/ma347.html>

A list of Poodle Rescue organizations on Adopt a Pet.
<http://www.adoptapet.com/s/adopt-a-poodle>

Florida Poodle Rescue.
<http://www.floridapoodlerescue.org>

Adopt a Rescued Poodle on **North Shore Animal League America.** <http://www.animalleague.org/adopt-a-pet/dogs/purebreed-rescue-adoption/poodle.html?referrer=https://www.google.com/>

United Kingdom Rescues:

Poodle Network UK. <http://www.poodlenetworkuk.org>

A list of Toy Poodle Rescues on **The Kennel Club (UK).** <http://www.thekennelclub.org.uk/services/public/findaresc ue/Default.aspx?breed=4099>

Little Dog Rescue. <http://www.littledogrescue.co.uk>

Toy Poodles on **dogsblog.com.**
<http://www.dogsblog.com/category/toy-poodle/>

How to Choose a Reputable Toy Poodle Breeder

If you far prefer purchasing a Toy Poodle puppy from a breeder, however, it would pay to be discriminating. Many will warn you that your choice of a breeder will have a long-lasting impact – after all, your Toy Poodle should ideally live for a long time. It is best to pick a responsible breeder who follows responsible breeding practices in the selection of breeding pair, the care of the mother and the puppies, and of course, the proper health checks and screenings.

Even if no breeder can give you a 100% health guarantee on their puppies, being handed a document attesting to health screenings ensures that you are dealing with a breeder who cared enough for the dogs' health. You don't want to be given vague promises of healthy puppies only later to find out that your puppy has a life-threatening disease. Avoid this potentially heartbreaking situation in the first place taking the time to choose carefully in the beginning. Besides, you will want some time to cultivate relations with the breeder, too – it is always a good idea to be in touch with someone who has some level of expertise in the care and raising of Toy Poodle dogs.

You might want to check out a listing of breeders registered with the AKC – look for one closest to your area.

Make a list, and begin reaching out. Once you do contact them, start a conversation regarding Toy Poodles and the likelihood that you might adopt. You'll be surprised at how much you can tell about the breeder from a conversation alone. Genuine passion for the breed is difficult to fake, and when you begin asking questions about their breeding programs and the Toy Poodles that they have in residence, their experience as breeders, and about the most recent litter they have produced, they should be willing and open to discussing these matters to you. This is a good idea to ask some general questions about the breed itself, especially if you are a first time dog owner and are unsure about whether your lifestyle is conducive to one of these dogs.

Be prepared, however, to answer questions asked of you, too. Remember that the breeder is also screening you as you are screening the breeder. Any responsible breeder will want to place their puppies in loving homes where they can be sure the new owners will take care of the little ones.

Your level of comfort in having these discussions with the breeder is also important – you will probably find yourself contacting the breeder again throughout the Toy Poodle's life – particularly in the beginning when you are still trying to figure out how best to take care of them. Open and good communication between yourself and the breeder is a good starting point, and warrants further exploration.

If you do feel comfortable speaking with the breeder, try to schedule a visit to their premises. The breeder will understand that you wish to see their facilities, and probably make the acquaintance of at least one of their breeding pair. Once there, just look around and observe. Do the dogs look healthy and happy? Are their living arrangements clean and nurturing? How does the breeder deal with their dogs? Don't hesitate to ask questions if you have any.

Once you have made up your mind, it is time to begin talking about the details. Some breeders will require a deposit or reservation fee for a puppy – you'll find that reputable breeders usually have an admirable line of customers wanting to purchase their puppies. Sign any contracts that are necessary, and simply settle in to wait for the puppies to be ready for you.

Tips for Selecting a Healthy Toy Poodle Puppy

As long as you are confident that you have picked a responsible breeder, you can pretty much rest assured that whichever puppy you pick will be just as healthy as all the rest. But some things to look out for when you are looking over the litter would be a sturdy, compact little body, a clean and shiny coat, clear eyes and nose without any discharge, clean ears, and a lively, energetic behavior which demonstrates a healthy curiosity about you and the rest of his littermates.

You might want to be a little more careful when choosing in terms of temperament, however. It may seem easy to just pick whichever puppy pushes his way towards you first, as this might mean a sort of bond or interest in you as his prospective owner, and what person doesn't want that? But a puppy showing extreme assertiveness early on in life might mean a temperamentally assertive or aggressive dog as he grows. Some would argue choosing the quiet, confident but friendly puppy instead. Of course, the actual choice depends on you and which dog you think would suit you best. If you want an assertive dog that seems naturally inclined to charm everyone and desires attention, then choose that puppy. If you'd rather have a quiet but friendly puppy, however, choose the quiet one – though you'll probably have some work cut out for you on breaking through any shyness issues he may have. Perhaps the best thing would be to first figure out what it is precisely that you are looking for in a lifelong companion. This should guide you as you make your individual choice.

Puppy-Proofing Your Home

You will probably need to take a little more care in puppy-proofing your home in preparation to bringing home a toy dog, as opposed to puppy-proofing for a larger breed. Of course, puppies in general are energetic and lively creatures, and you will want to make sure that their natural curiosity will not lead them into accidents or injuries at home. But Toy Poodles can be even more demanding – this is a lively, energetic and agile breed, so you might want to check over your house again to see if there are any other tempting but dangerous possibilities that a lively Toy Poodle puppy can get into.

Puppy-proofing, as most experts will tell you, is not unlike baby-proofing. In the beginning, you will probably want to confine your puppy to at least one room in the house, but it should be expected that eventually, your dog will also gain access to the rest of the house. Give their designated room a thorough once-over, and then check the other areas of the house to make sure that there is nothing that could potentially be dangerous to your Toy Poodle.

Things to watch out for include:

- Power or electrical cords – these can seem like tempting chew toys to puppies, and you don't want them inadvertently getting electrocuted. Secure any electrical cords, and tuck them out of reach.
- Keep dangerous items around the house like knives, scissors and other sharp objects out of harm's way. Best to put them away in a secure drawer as opposed

to leaving them out on a table, for instance, where there would still be a risk that these might fall to the ground.

- Watch out for small items that can be swallowed by a puppy such as tiny buttons, coins, paper clips, rubber bands, and other similar objects. Otherwise you'll be making an impromptu trip to emergency in order to get that blockage out of your dog's throat.

- Be conscientious in cleaning up after yourself – and the rest of your family should do the same. Used cotton swabs, tissues, shampoos, and other items that can carry strange scents to a dog should be thrown away in a secure garbage bin.

- Put away precious items and important documents. If it's valuable – put it away and out of your dog's reach. You don't want them breaking an expensive vase, attempting to chew on your phone or tablet, or messing up your child's homework, or even important work documents that you labored on for weeks.

- Secure open sources of water such as the toilet bowl and other water drums. Water can be quite tempting for Toy Poodles – they are descended from Poodles that were excellent water retrievers. But Toy Poodles are small enough that getting trapped in a large enough container of water – whether clean or otherwise - can drown them.

- Secure curtain cords and long-hanging curtains from off the ground. These playful puppies could get it into their heads to wrestle with things that drape all the way to the ground. Sure, they can entertain themselves for hours this way, but do you really want the ends of your curtains chewed on? Not to mention the very distinct possibility that these puppies can strangle themselves as they go around and around the cords.

- Remove poisonous plants. If you aren't sure whether or not the decorative plant in your living room is poisonous, best to put it away until you can verify whether or not it is. While you're at it, put away cleaning items and other chemical solutions that could potentially be toxic or lethal to a puppy.

- Make sure that your food items are safely stored up and away from the reach of these puppies. Do the same thing with the garbage cans, too. Not only is it likely that these puppies will make quite a mess, but you don't want them ingesting anything that isn't good for them, either.

There are probably a few more things in your home that you should secure or put away – many owners actually get down on their hands and knees and try to see their home as a puppy would, just to make sure. Be conscientious in cleaning up after yourself, and ask the rest of your household to be the same, too. Be vigilant – remember that it is always better to err on the side of caution!

Chapter Four: Caring for Your New Toy Poodle

Bringing a new Toy Poodle home can be an exciting time, but it can also be fraught with a number of unique challenges. For one thing, your puppy will find himself in a completely new and strange environment, surrounded by people who are practically complete strangers. You can probably expect a bit of barking or whining in the earlier days. However, there are a few things you can do to help ease the transition – including providing them a comfortable and secure sleeping area, and settling them into a regular exercise and grooming routine as soon as possible.

Once they have settled into their new home and to your lifestyle, they should do fine. Toy Poodles are quite versatile – they can do quite well as apartment dogs, but they will do equally well in a house with a yard or at a farm. Just remember that toy dogs can be pretty fragile – considering their physical size, as well as their propensity for high-energy activities. Make sure that they will be safe from potential injuries or accidents within their immediate surroundings.

Habitat and Exercise Requirements for Toy Poodles

It is imperative that you begin crate training your Toy Poodle as soon as possible – you need to provide him with a space of his own in which he feels safe and comfortable, a kind of den that gives him space for privacy and quiet. Make this crate as appealing as possible for him by furnishing it appropriately with beddings, dog toys, and perhaps a treat or two to keep him occupied while he is in his own space.

Allowing your Toy Poodle to sleep on furniture or on your bed is not really advisable. First of all, not everybody in the household might appreciate having a dog sleep in bed with them. Second, puppies will tend to sleep a lot – on the average, some 15-20 hours per day. Granted that they will be quite energetic little puppies when awake, but this means that they will need sufficient resting time. Even as they grow older, their sleeping hours will still be quite long, around 13 hours for adolescent and adult Toy Poodles, and plenty of naps for senior dogs. It is important to provide him with a sleeping area that is quiet and free of disturbances to give him plenty of time to get a snooze.

In the beginning, you might want to keep the crate close in your room at night to allow the dog to adjust to his new sleeping arrangements, and being in your company at night can do just that. You will want to wean him away from this gradually, however, to allow him to develop a measure of self-confidence and avoid the development of separation anxiety issues – which can grow to become frustrating long-term. Begin training them early, and this should definitely include crate training.

Exercise Requirements for Toy Poodles

Toy Poodles are an active, intelligent, agile, and fun-loving breed, so it is important that they be provided with enough mental and physical stimulation to keep them happy and healthy. But how much exercise should you give them? It might be too easy to underestimate this breed's capacity for activity given their small size and delicate appearance. But the truth is, at their best, Toy Poodles can be quite the little gymnasts!

Of course, you wouldn't want to over-exert your Toy Poodle, either, and this is why determining a good exercise routine is advisable. To begin with, you might want to ask your vet for their input, as well as what particular types of activities would be great for this tiny dog.

Providing them with enough physical and mental stimulation also ensure that their vast energy goes to something productive. They have a lot of energy to spare – whether physical or mental – and this will need to be channeled to something challenging and positive. Otherwise, deprived of enough avenues for activity, all that pent-up energy can quickly turn to destructive behavior. And not only will regular activities with your pet improve your relationship with each other, there are myriad health benefits for your Toy Poodle, too – better socialization skills, better sleep, improved overall mood, and the reduction of undesirable behavior such as excessive barking or attention seeking.

For such a tiny dog, low impact, regular exercise is best. Daily walking on a leash and harness is recommended. An hour's worth of exercise for adult Toy Poodles is a good average, which you can break up in shorter walks throughout the day to keep it as low impact as possible. Occasionally, you might want to vary this with some play or games instead – particularly when walking outdoors is not feasible. Make sure that he has enough running room inside the house without being in any danger of bumping into things or having things fall on him. Despite the occasional play, however, walking is still the best exercise recommended for Toy Poodles – it gives them an opportunity to get out of the house, explore the world, develop their social skills, and satisfy their curiosity.

If you are still worried that your Toy Poodle is either not getting enough exercise, or getting too much exercise, you should just adjust accordingly. Let your dog teach you what is a good average exercise time for him – if he seems lethargic and tired at the end of the day, perhaps you need to lessen his walks a little bit. If, on the other hand, he is still quite assertive at the end of the day, with plenty of energy left over to bark at anything and everything – then perhaps he hasn't had enough chance to release all that energy. At all times, make sure that your dog is properly fed and has regular veterinary checkups to ensure his capacity for regular exercise and physical exertion.

Chapter Five: Meeting Your Toy Poodle's Nutritional Needs

A good diet and proper, balanced nutrition is essential to keeping your Toy Poodle healthy and happy. Much as with humans, what dogs eat can go a long way to keeping your dog free of illnesses or diseases, and in providing him enough energy to meet his daily needs.

For small breeds such as the Toy Poodle, you should pick out commercially available dog food that is specific to small breed dogs. And yes, there is a difference – as opposed to dog food for larger breeds. Smaller dog breeds usually have high metabolic rates, and they need more calories far more frequently than larger dogs. In fact, it is probably best to space out your Toy Poodle's diet over small or moderate portions spread over three or four hours each day. This way, they can quickly replenish the nutrients from their last meal – which they can quickly burn through in a matter of hours. And if you are taking your Toy Poodle out for a walk, it might also be a good idea to bring along some snacks or treats for your dog to prevent possible cases of hypoglycemia. If you notice your Toy Poodle showing signs of weakness or lethargy, for instance, then you can probably spread out his meals a bit more over the day to keep him from going without meals for too long.

Throughout this chapter, you'll find more information regarding the nutritional needs of your dog, picking quality dog food, and some general tips on feeding your Toy Poodle.

The Nutritional Needs of Dogs

All dogs require a balanced diet with the necessary vitamins, minerals and nutrients that his body needs. Below are the essential nutrients that are considered important for a dog's optimal health. In addition, in order to keep him well-hydrated, you might also want to offer him a readily accessible bowl of fresh water in a spill-proof container. In fact, many recommend steering clear of dry kibble for Toy Poodles – and the larger kinds of kibbles might be particularly difficult for them to digest. You will want plenty of real meat and fat in their diet, so choose accordingly.

Proteins

Mainly obtained from meat and most meat-based products, protein is essential for growth and cell regeneration and repair, and for Toy Poodles especially, are necessary to help maintain their coat or fur. Be aware that experts do not recommend feeding your dog raw eggs, as this may have actually be harmful to their health.

Carbohydrates

This is usually derived from fiber-based products, and help in maintaining the intestinal health of your pet. Some carbohydrates can even be a good source of energy for your pet.

Fats

Fats provide your pet with a concentrated source of energy, and are also essential for some vitamins (A, E, D and K) to be absorbed. They help in protecting the internal organs and are vital in cellular production.

Vitamins and Minerals

Vitamins and minerals usually cannot be synthesized by a dog's body, so the primary source of these are the synthesized versions obtainable in commercially available quality dog foods. Vitamins and minerals help in the normal functioning of their bodies, and also helps maintain their bones and teeth.

How to Select a High-Quality Dog Food Brand

We already pointed out the necessity of choosing dog food that is breed-size specific, or food that has been specially formulated for smaller dog breeds, and why this makes a difference. We have also recommended selecting moist or canned food over dry kibble as preferable for smaller dogs such as the Toy Poodle.

And yet even this narrowing down still leaves us with a wide variety of dog food to choose from. How do you know which is best? First of all, you're going to have to learn how to read the label.

Ideally, the label on the dog food should already tell you everything you need to know – you just need to look for it. First of all, look for food specially formulated for small breed dogs, and then look for the AAFCO statement of nutritional adequacy. Next, check the ingredients list.

What you are looking for is meat-based dog food, which you can recognize by reading the first few ingredients on the list. While dogs are essentially omnivores, in their natural state they will still prefer meat instead of vegetables, and their diet should reflect this accordingly. The first few ingredients on the list represent the greater components of the dog food because manufacturers are required by law to list product ingredients in descending order, based on their pre-cooked weights. You are looking for a meat-based diet, so real meats such as chicken, lamb, or fish listed as the top ingredients is a good sign. Be wary of meat byproducts – you want quality protein for your dog, and meat byproducts do not always provide the same nutrition as real meat. Look for whole grains such as rice instead of fillers such as corn or wheat. And finally, avoid artificial preservatives and coloring whenever you can,

It is quite possible that you might have to change dog food brands throughout your dog's lifetime – sometimes they may just get bored from eating the same thing every day, or sometimes they just hanker for something new and different. Or perhaps you find your dog becoming lethargic and weak, and suspect that they might not be getting enough nutrition from their food. Learning how to read the labels of commercially available dog food is a skill that you will definitely need in caring for your Toy Poodle. Just remember to implement dietary changes slowly – give your dog's stomach time to adjust to the new food, rather than just changing foods directly, lest you cause stomach upsets or indigestion. When in doubt, don't hesitate to consult with your veterinarian.

Tips for Feeding Your Toy Poodle

As mentioned above, small dogs such as the Toy Poodle require more calories per pound/kilo compared to large dogs – and with a high metabolism, with a general rule of some 40 calories per pound. Some 22-32% of proteins and 1-20% of fats in their food is a good estimate.

Because these tiny dogs can burn through their meals quite quickly given their high metabolism, you will want to carefully space their meals throughout the day. For puppies, free feeding may be a good idea, as long as you make sure that their food is kept clean and fresh at all times. You can gradually begin implementing small meals around 3-5 times throughout the day. Stick to a regular schedule as much as possible – not only will this help them behaviorally, but it can be a good foundation for housebreaking your dog. And of course, regular feeding will help ensure your dog's health and wellbeing.

Again, make sure that your Toy Poodle is kept well-hydrated. Aside from the moisture that he gets from his food, provide him with a ready source of clean water at all times in a spill-proof container. If you are having difficulties determining what is a good meal portion for your pet, or if you think he isn't getting all the nutrients he needs and may need to shift to a different kind or brand of dog food – speak to your veterinarian first and get his professional opinion. You will probably find yourself shifting brands throughout your Poodle's lifetime anyway – should your dog seek a little variety and lose interest in his current dog food. And as always, always implement dietary changes – even if it is just a shift from one brand to another – gradually, in order to give your dog's stomach time to adjust.

Dangerous Foods to Avoid

Some Toy Poodles might show a certain preference for human food in addition to their regular diet. This is not always a bad thing, but indiscriminate feeding can sometimes be dangerous. Not everything that is edible to humans is equally edible to canines. In fact, some people foods can be downright dangerous, even fatal, to our four-legged friends.

Below is a list of some of the dangerous that you should, in no instance, feed to your Toy Poodle. Should it happen that he ingests one or more of the following, bring him to the nearest emergency services immediately.

- Alcohol
- Apple seeds
- Avocado
- Cherry pits
- Chocolate
- Citrus
- Coconut
- Coffee
- Garlic
- Grapes/raisins
- Hops
- Macadamia nuts
- Milk and Dairy
- Mold
- Mushrooms
- Mustard seeds
- Onions/leeks
- Peach pits
- Potato leaves/stems
- Raw meat and eggs
- Rhubarb leaves
- Salty snacks
- Tea
- Tomato leaves/stems
- Walnuts
- Xylitol
- Yeast dough

Chapter Six: Training Your Toy Poodle

The training of your dog can prove to be one of the most rewarding aspects of your relationship with your Toy Poodle. They are an extremely intelligent breed, loyal, good-natured, and with a beautiful temperament to match. They can match any training you give them with the enthusiasm to back up their keen intelligence. You might be surprised at how quickly they can pick up the various tricks and behaviors you teach them. Or not – after all, you know your Poodle best.

Training your Toy Poodle is one thing that must not be skimped on. Sometimes, it can be easy to accept toy breeds as nothing more than lapdogs, and to leave it at that. But the Toy Poodles come from a long line of working dogs that have served mankind faithfully for many years. An intelligent dog should be given enough physical and mental stimulation – not to mention affection – to match their natural inclinations. Otherwise, all that pent up energy can easily turn destructive.

While not all Toy Poodles are the same – each dog is unique and individual – there are breed-specific characteristics that define the Poodle. Aside from their intelligence, Toy Poodles are also quite sensitive and will not respond well to harsh training. They are also proud dogs, and will not appreciate being humiliated or given confusing commands. And Toy Poodles also have keen curiosity and boundless energy that needs to be directed and nurtured into proper behavioral training. Their natural athletic abilities also make them crave physical exercises that can challenge and develop their natural agility.

Socializing Your New Toy Poodle Puppy

Proper training of any dog requires proper socialization while they are still puppies. You want them to develop a healthy curiosity about the world and a good trust in you as the owner, without the fear, timidity or shyness that can characterize puppies that have never been taught the proper socialization skills. On the other extreme, you might end up with an aggressive and high strung puppy that grows up to be a neurotic little dog. This must be avoided at all costs – the difference is a happy home environment and a well-adjusted, confident, and lovable canine companion. The time spent on training – even if you don't find it fun, which would be the rare instance – will be well worth it.

Socialization skills must be taught early – within the first six months – preferably from 7 to 16 weeks old. Experts consider this a critical learning period when the puppy apparently makes up its mind as to how to regard humans, objects, and other animals. After this critical period, their behavior "sets" – and it would be difficult, if not impossible, to make a neurotic, shy, or fearful puppy change its worldview. Make the most of this early time to teach your dog socialization skills – the repercussions would be a lifetime of continuous stress at every new and strange thing, person, or animal.

Teaching the Toy Poodle puppy socialization skills is not that difficult. He would already have started to learn as he deals with his mother and his littermates. The first thing you would want to do then is to get him accustomed to your presence, and to being handled by you and other humans.

Begin with short touches or brief periods in his company each day. As he becomes more comfortable with you, try to broaden his experience a little bit more by exposing him to the handling and presence of other people – family members or friends who would be willing to briefly and gently handle your Toy Poodle puppy. The more he gets used to being handled by different people, to better his socialization skills will be.

Socialization does not stop with childhood or adulthood. True socialization can last a dog's lifetime – but it can be as simple as exposing him to something new everyday. Properly supervised, you can allow him to explore the rooms of the house, the yard, or take him out on a collar and harness for a brief walk around the neighborhood – where the two of you might bump into another person or another dog or cat. Once he realizes that there is nothing to fear from these strange creatures, or from the outside world, the better he can make the necessary mental adjustment to living in the stimuli-filled life of his human family. You will also want him to be in the proper mental framework for further training – which means that he needs to grow to trust you as his owner. Spend as much time with him while he is young and you'll have the loyalty and willingness to please of your beloved Toy Poodle

Crate Training - Housebreaking Your Puppy

You will probably need to confine your puppy before he is housebroken so that he does not pee and poop all over the house. This is what makes crate training so popular – and so effective – for many dog owners. Not only does it keep him from creating accidents all over the place – this can also help you create a routine for your dog which he should easily pick up. In fact, Toy Poodles are, if anything, creatures of habit. Once it becomes obvious to them that you intend for something to become a regular routine, they will actually begin to expect it as a routine.

Crate training works on the principle that dogs will not like to pee or poop in the same place where they sleep. In order to foster this as a behavior, the crate should become a comfortable den for them – and the constant and regular periods out of the crate will be the time that they can go to the bathroom.

Pick a well-sized crate and equip it for your Toy Poodle – give him comfortable beddings, a spill proof water container, some treats, and maybe a few toys, and begin by getting him accustomed to being inside the crate. Creating the association of the crate as a comfortable and safe space for him also has another advantage – it teaches your dog that it is okay for him to be confined and alone for brief periods of time. You might begin by keeping him inside the crate for a few seconds at first, and gradually increase the time he spends inside as his comfort level grows. Be sure to lavish him with praise for doing this – and soon he will willingly enough go inside the crate without too much prompting on your part. Then you can begin to leave him in the crate as you step into another room – again starting with a few seconds to begin with, and gradually working your way to longer and longer periods of time. A wonderful advantage of this method is that it helps to keep your dog from developing separation anxiety issues – a common enough dilemma for toy breeds as a whole.

When your Toy Poodle is happy enough to stay within the crate for long periods of time, begin to instill a regular schedule – both for eating and for going out to relieve himself. Here, patience and constancy is key. Providing him with a regular schedule out of the den – ideally during those times when you might expect him to be ready to poop or pee – is ideal. This is variable, of course, but generally, after eating, after exercise, after play, immediately in the morning, and before you yourself go to bed, are good times to bring your puppy outside to relieve himself. You might want to adjust this depending on your dog's unique quirks. And remember to bring him to the same place to relieve himself at all times – whether a specific corner in the yard or to a puppy pad. When he does go when he's outside the crate, be sure to reward him and praise him lavishly for it. Doing this will help to reinforce the desired behavior.

Inevitably, there will be some accidents – especially in the beginning. When this happens, don't get angry. Remember that your puppy is still learning – and it may seem strange to him to be punished for something as natural as peeing or pooping. Not to mention that Toy Poodles are sensitive by nature, and will not react well to harsh treatment. You might express your disapproval in a firm voice and then withdraw your affection for a time. Just be sure to do this immediately upon or immediately after the undesirable behavior. This would allow him to create the appropriate connection. If you only punish him after you find the trails of his misdeeds, which might be hours after the fact, you'll only end up confusing him as to what he is being punished for.

Given the natural intelligence and eagerness to please of the Toy Poodle breed, it probably won't take him too long to figure out what you expect of him. Just remember to practice patience and consistency – even if it does take him some time to put things together.

Positive Reinforcement and Rewards for Obedience

There are a lot of tricks you can teach your Toy Poodle – you'll be amazed at how many commands he can learn. Whether you are housebreaking or teaching your Toy Poodle tricks, however, you must remember that a positive approach always works best. The Toy Poodle's nature is sensitive, and will not respond well to anything less. In this vein, positive reinforcement training entails the use of encourage, praise, a pat, a scratch behind the ears, or other forms of rewards for training.

You may want to give some time to leash training, as Toy Poodles can be quite a little energy ball while walking, despite the leash. And aside from housebreaking and teaching basic commands such as Come, Sit, Stay, etc., you will also devote some time to addressing potential behavior problems such as excessive barking, whining, or chewing on furniture. In this, positive reinforcement can also be used – by rewarding a different behavior instead. For instance, using a chew toy instead of chewing furniture should be rewarded, sitting and waiting quietly rather than barking at the door before it is opened, or peeing and pooping in his designated spot rather than indoors – or elsewhere, for that matter. As with housebreaking, patience and consistency is the key.

All in all, a well trained Toy Poodle can be a joy and a delight to have in the house – but this mainly lies on your efforts to train him. Not only will proper training make for a less stressful household, the time you spend training your dog will also nurture the relationship you have with each other. Just remember to keep it light and fun – if he has had enough of training one day, just return to it the next day. Don't force him to train – or this will create bad associations. Though for Toy Poodles, their intelligence naturally has them seeking some form of mental stimulation, so making a game or a fun activity of your training sessions will probably be your best bet.

Chapter Seven: Grooming Your Toy Poodle

While grooming your Toy Poodle does require some work – it is not impossible to learn. Of course, you can pay for a professional groomer to do all the work for you, but it is always a good idea to get a hand in and learn some of the basics yourself. Not only does this facilitate greater bonding between you and your pet, it can also save you money, as grooming costs will add up after a time. In time, you'll probably surprise yourself at how easy and fun it can be!

The Toy Poodle's coat is one of the reasons why the breed is popular among some owners – a hypoallergenic and no-shedding coat can make Toy Poodles the ideal companion for those suffering from allergies or respiratory problems. But despite this advantage, the breed's coat does require regular grooming. They might not shed, but they do lose hair, and the very tight, dense and curly coat will need to be brushed regularly to get rid of the loose hair. They will also need a regular haircut – a Toy Poodle's coat is unlike the fur of most dogs, and is more similar to human hair that will not stop growing. Depending on which type of Poodle clip or cut you prefer, such clipping will also need to be done regularly in order to maintain their coat's appearance.

When the Toy Poodle is young, their hair is still quite soft, and may either be curly or wavy. As they grow, however, so does their hair. There is generally a coat change sometime between 9 and 18 months as the puppy matures. During this time, the need for grooming and brushing also increases if only to keep your dog from becoming matted.

This chapter contains some lessons to guide you on how often to groom your Toy Poodle, what you will need, and how to proceed.

Recommended Tools to Have on Hand

More than with any other dog breed, it is a good idea to invest in quality grooming equipment for your Toy Poodle. You will be using these regularly, and cheap or poor quality tools can actually ruin your dog's coat. Besides, given how often you will be grooming your little high maintenance companion, you'll want grooming tools that will stand regular and long-term use as much as possible.

- Curved slicker brush – for areas of short hair
- Rubber tipped pin brush with a cushioned pad – for areas of the coat that are medium to long in length, as well as the curly hairs of the coat
- Two sided steel comb – for the face, as well as to check the coat for tangles
- Serrated de-matting comb – can find and remove tangles and knots
- Clippers and scissors set – for various clips and cuts all over the coat
- Basic scissors with blunt, rounded ends – to tidy up the coat and to clip around the eyes
- Grooming table
- Nail clipper or grinder
- Eye wipes
- Nose balm
- Paw wax
- Dog shampoo and conditioner
- Oil spray or finishing spray/coat dressing

Tips for Bathing and Grooming Toy Poodles

The bedrock for a well-groomed Toy Poodle is regular brushing. Most groomers actually recommend brushing your dog *before* bathing him – nothing can be more frustrating than working with a knot or tangle that is wet. Bathing can be done as often as once a week to once a month – depending on how dirty your Toy Poodle gets. Brushing and regular grooming, however, should be done more regularly – some dedicated owners give their Toy Poodles a brush at least once a day. If that is not feasible for you, then 2-3 times a week is a good habit.

You can use a grooming table if you have one – or some other feasible alternative. The purpose of daily or regular grooming is to remove loose or fallen hair which has gotten tangled in the coat – Poodles may not shed, but they do lose hair, and these can get caught in the tight curls, thereby creating mats. Using a pin brush or a slicker brush, give your Poodle a once-over regularly just to get those loose hair out. You may use a light spritz of conditioner or detangler to make things easier – and this can also help prevent hair from breaking. Too much brushing might also cause static and fly-always from forming, so a bit of misting is a good idea.

Brush in sections – working your way through the entire coat, making sure you have gotten all the tangles out. Use a hand to hold a section of hair before brushing – this keeps you from pulling on the hair, which might be painful for your dog. Some recommend using an oil spray that you work completely into the coat – all the way down to the skin – if you know that you will not be able to brush your dog's coat again for a few days.

When bathing, use quality dog shampoo and conditioner, making sure that you don't get any of the products into his eyes. Rinse thoroughly, making sure to get all of the shampoo out – any leftover shampoo will dry and irritate his skin. Once your Toy Poodle is thoroughly clean, use a dryer set on low heat and a brush for his curls to dry him. Don't let him air dry as this can actually tighten the curls, making subsequent brushing more difficult, and any tangles more difficult to get out.

Finish up with eye wipes to keep your Poodle's face clean of tear stains, and a nose balm to protect his nose from the sun, drying, or chapping. Some groomers also recommend using paw wax to prevent dry, cracked paws.

As for clipping – it is always a good idea to have a professional groomer give your Toy Poodle your preferred clip to begin with, then you can simply trim every so often to maintain this cut. There are a number of popular Poodle clips you can choose from – with a greater range than that which the AKC considers acceptable. Always be careful when trimming around or near the eyes, ears, and paws so that you don't injure them. If in doubt, don't. Better leave it up to the groomer the next time you pay them a visit. Just be sure to keep their coat well-maintained with regular brushing and combing.

Other Grooming Tasks

Cleaning Your Toy Poodle's Ears

Like with most dog breeds with low-hanging ears that contain an abundance of hair, it is advisable to pluck the hair inside the ear canals to allow for better air circulation. The inside of the ears should also be checked and cleaned regularly – moisture that has been trapped inside the ears can become fertile ground for bacterial infection, so it is always best to stay on top of ear cleaning.

Use a moistened cotton swab to clean out the inner ears gently. Try not to go down to deep into his ear – a dog's ears are quite sensitive and you will not want to cause him any injury. Q-tips are not recommended as the ends can poke your dog's sensitive inner ears.

Trimming Your Toy Poodle's Nails

You can use a dog nail clipper or a grinder to address your Toy Poodle's nails that have grown too long. Depending on your comfort level, you can work easily with a clipper or a grinder – trimming or filing down the nails that have begun clacking on the floorboards.

This is another important part of grooming, and should not be skipped. Too-long nails could get caught on clothes or carpets, and may even make walking or running difficult or painful for your dog once the nails start pushing back up against the paw. This can eventually lead to lameness or injury.

Cut conservatively – especially if it is your first time. Best to have a professional groomer or a vet show you how it's done first. The important thing is not to cut the quick – a vessel that supplies blood to the nails, or you might cause some bleeding. Should you nick your dog, however, some styptic powder can help staunch the bleeding.

Brushing Your Toy Poodle's Teeth

Regular dental care is another important part of your grooming session – it keeps down tooth decay, bleeding gums, and so forth. And yes, dogs are just as prone to this as humans are. Use soft toothbrush and dog toothpaste to brush your Toy Poodle's teeth – starting them out while they are young is a good way to build this habit into them. Brush gently and carefully. And remember to be patient. If your puppy gets to squirming, just let him go and try again another day. You will want to keep his association with teeth brushing – and grooming – as positive as possible until he grows so used to it that he might even enjoy having his teeth brushed!

Chapter Eight: Breeding Your Toy Poodle

Responsible breeders and international kennel clubs such as the AKC have long recognized the value of breeding to improve the breed. Responsible breedership means being driven to propagate the best of a dog breed, and if possible, breeding out potential weaknesses, illnesses or disease from a dog's lines. Breeding responsibly, therefore, means not just breeding for profit, or even being irresponsible enough to allow the breeding of dogs despite having been diagnosed with congenital flaws or illnesses.

There are many, unfortunately, who breed because of the income they might derive from the puppies – particularly for purebreds like Toy Poodles that generally do command a higher price in the market. But the truth is that breeding dogs will require a lot time, effort, energy, and even financial investment – including the need to learn a lot about the process and about the specific breed. If you are only in it for the money, it is questionable whether the monetary equivalent of all that would even have you breaking even. On the other hand, if you are driven by a genuine passion and dedication to the breed, then the experience can be extremely worthwhile.

Where do you begin? Most would recommend showing your dog and attending dog shows. This is a great place to network with other breeders and to learn more about what makes a great Toy Poodle. You learn about their possible illnesses, the best way to exercise and feed them, and to train them. Knowing as much as you can about a breed is one of the best starting points towards responsible dog breeding.

Basic Dog Breeding Information

The first step is a careful selection of your breeding stud and the dam. You will want to choose a breeding pair with qualities that you want them to pass on to their offspring – whether it be coat color, coat type, intelligence, or even temperament. But the most important thing is to choose a breeding pair that have been checked out by a veterinarian and who have undergone all the necessary health screenings. The Poodle Club of America (PCA), in fact, recommends that Toy Poodles undergo screenings for the following prior to breeding:

- Progressive Retinal Atrophy (PRA) DNA test (with an OFA approved laboratory)
- Eye Exam by a boarded ACVO Ophthalmologist (with the results to be registered with the OFA or CERF)
- Patellar Luxation (OFA Evaluation)

It is just as important, too, to stay updated with the latest medical and veterinary news regarding canine health – scientists are working hard to isolate carriers and develop screening tests for other possible illnesses to which Toy Poodles may be prone to.

The AKC also recommends a good grounding in genetics – including a careful study of both of the lines of your breeding pair. For instance, why does the dam look more like its father than its mother, or why do certain desirable traits skip a generation? Always be careful to make informed choices regarding which breeding pair to use, and why. Once you have made your selection and finalized a stud contract, bring each of the dogs to a vet for a thorough pre-breeding examination by a vet. Her vaccinations should be current, she should be in good health and condition, of the proper age, and she should be clear of parasites.

For Toy Poodles, one other thing to keep in mind as you select your breeding pair is their height. There are three types of recognized Poodles: Standard, Miniature, and Toy. Nobody really knows how Toy Poodles came about, but the theory is that they were simply a "bred down" version of the Standard Poodle – presumably, a result of breeding smaller Poodles with each other. Keep in mind, however, that the only real distinction of a Toy Poodle is its height – and must be 10 inches or under. For most kennel clubs, a Poodle taller than 6 inches is no longer considered a Toy Poodle. By contrast, a Miniature Poodle has a height of 15 inches or under at the highest point of the shoulders, while a Standard Poodle stands at a height of over 15 inches. Other than these height differences, all three types are still recognized as one breed.

Now that you have these preliminaries down, let's take a closer look at what it actually means to breed Toy Poodles. It all starts with the female heat cycle – which in Toy Poodles can begin as early as 6 months, though the typical range can be anywhere from 4 to 7 months. Your Poodle's heat cycle is central to dog breeding because it is during this time that she becomes fertile and able to become pregnant. It must be stated, however, that breeding during the dam's first heat is never done. She needs enough time to grow mentally and physically to prepare for the rigors of pregnancy and motherhood – which is why most breeders wait until the Toy Poodle is at least two years old before breeding. In the meantime, care should be taken that no unplanned pregnancies occur. Needless to say, if you are not planning to breed your dog – especially if your dog has been diagnosed with a congenital disease of some sort, then spaying is highly recommended. Doing so may actually prevent some serious health conditions from developing in the first place, such as ovarian and mammary cancer and other infections.

While all dogs are different, most will go through two heat cycles each year, or every six months, each one lasting anywhere from two to four weeks. During this time, there are four stages that a female dog will go through. The four stages of heat generally include:

- Proestrus – The beginning of the heat cycle and is characterized by noticeable signs such as a swollen vulva and a bloody vaginal discharge. During this time, she will not yet be ready to mate. This stage can last anywhere from 4 to 15 days.
- Estrus – The second stage, which can last from 5-8 days. You will know she has entered estrus when she is finally be receptive to a male. This is the time when she is fertile and the chances of pregnancy are good.

- Diestrus – This stage can last from 60-90 days, and will happen whether or not the pregnancy was successful. If not, cases of "false pregnancy" may occur, when her body mimics the symptoms of pregnancy, but will not actually be pregnant.
- Anestrus – The last and final stage, this is really just the time when the heat cycle is ending and her body is returning to normal. This can last from 3-4 months, during which no sexual activity takes place.

You will, of course, have to bring the dam and the stud together during her estrus period – which you can anticipate by watching out for the signs of heat during Proestrus. While they may not mate during Proestrus, some breeders allow time for brief socialization between them, in order to make them more comfortable with each other.

Some breeders recommend the first mating to take place between the 10th and 14th day after the onset of Proestrus. Mating again every other day after that may help ensure a successful pregnancy – as long as she still accepts the male. Some two or three matings will therefore take place.

The process itself is pretty straightforward – the male will mount the female from the back, and after some rapid pelvic thrusts, there will be penetration and ejaculation. Afterwards, the male may move around so that they are positioned rear to rear, during which they will be connected for some 10 to 30 minutes. This is known as a "tie," and is the result of the swelling of the bulbus glandis of the penis. Leave them be when this happens – they will separate naturally after some time, while forcing them to separate may actually injure one or both of them.

Pregnancy and Whelping

A pregnancy can be confirmed at around 28 days by a vet through abdominal palpitation or ultrasound or x-rays. This is the only time you can be sure of a successful pregnancy, given that even the signs of pregnancy that she may be showing may actually be the result of a false pregnancy. Canine gestation lasts approximately 63 days – and once pregnancy is confirmed, you should prepare yourself to take good care of your pregnant Poodle.

Consult with your vet regarding the best ways of doing this – which will most involve:

- Regular but moderate exercise
- Good nutrition and a gradual increase in food intake towards the latter weeks of her pregnancy, as her body weight also increases.
- Prepare a whelping box and allow her to get accustomed to this a few weeks before her expected date of labor. Place the whelping box in a clean place that affords her some measure of privacy, but in

which she will not be subject to chills or drafts. Keep her box clean – many prefer to line this with newspaper for greater ease of cleaning after whelping. This box should be roomy enough for her and her expected puppies, with raised sides to keep the puppies from rolling out.

- Gather supplies you may need for the whelping, including clean towels, paper towels, un-waxed dental floss, iodine, scissors, and the number of your vet and emergency services just in case something goes wrong. Needless to say, the time when you're waiting for her to go into labor is a good time to read up and learn all you can about it. If this is your first time and you're feeling a little nervous, having an experienced breeder to guide you through the experience can be a good thing.

Shortly before she is about to go into labor, you will notice that her temperature will begin to drop – her normal temperatures are usually around 100 to 102.5, but this will fall to about 99 degrees or lower. When this happens, you can pretty much expect her to go into labor within the next 24 hours. Make sure to keep your schedule free during this time so that you can stay with her through this process.

Many dogs give birth naturally and without much issue. You will notice the arrival of each puppy preceded by panting and straining on the part of the expectant mother.

When the puppies arrive, they will each come with their own placenta, which the mother will tear off with her teeth. She will also chew off the umbilical cord, and will lick the puppy in order to stimulate breathing. Should she fail to do this – which can happen, especially if she is a first-time mother, you should be ready to step in and do what is necessary. The placenta should be removed as soon as possible lest the puppy suffocate, so be ready to tear this off. Use a soft towel to clean off mucus or fluids from the puppy's nose or mouth, and then gently rub them with the towel to stimulate breathing. The dental floss, on the other hand, can be used to tie off the umbilical cord prior to cutting. Do this about two inches away from the abdomen, and then use iodine on the cut end to prevent infection. Once the mother sees what is expected of her, you may find her gradually taking over her motherly duties quite willingly.

Make sure that the newborns are able to suckle from their mother as soon as possible – or soon after being born. This will allow them to ingest the colostrum, or their mother's first milk, which contains the antibodies which are produced just after birth. Since the puppies' immune system is still not developed at this time, it is essential that they get their mother's immunity through the milk – which will include protection against the diseases she has been vaccinated for. This is the reason why it is so important to have her vaccinated prior to breeding.

Most dog pregnancies should proceed naturally, and without any problems. Be aware though, of the following possible causes of concern. Should the following transpire, be sure to call your vet immediately:

- Signs of pain, trembling, shivering, or collapse
- If she passes a dark green or bloody fluid prior to the arrival of the first puppy (this is normal after the first puppy has been born)
- Strong contractions that have lasted for more than 45 minutes without any puppy being born
- More than two hours elapsing between the birth of puppies
- If there are still no signs of labor by the 64th day after her last mating

Weaning and Raising Puppies

The development of the puppies should proceed fairly quickly after they are born – initially, of course, they will be quite helpless, with ears and eyes closed, unable to walk or crawl, and without the capacity to regulate their own body temperatures.

It is imperative that you keep the puppies warm during this time – a chill can literally kill them. It is also imperative that you take care of the lactating mother, making sure that she is healthy and well able to provide her puppies with nourishing milk. At this time, the puppies' job is to nurse, sleep, and maybe learn some basic socialization skills with his littermates – until about 2 to 4 weeks when their senses start to develop. It would be around this time that you can begin to wean the puppies – or at around 3-4 weeks. You will be doing this gradually until the puppies are fully weaned – ideally at around 8 weeks. By this time, the mother's milk supply should have naturally dried off as well, as the puppies dependence on her milk supply is slowly replaced by the ability to eat food.

The important thing to remember whenever you begin changing a dog's diet – even that for puppies – is that the change must take place gradually, allowing their stomach and body to adjust a little at a time. To wean puppies, many recommend using a puppy formula using puppy food that you already intend to feed them later on. Moisten this with warm water or canine milk to create a kind of soupy gruel or slush, and offer this to them in a low pan that they can easily reach.

They will still be nursing at this time, but their curiosity may lead them to investigate the contents of the pan. If they need some encouragement, you can try dipping a finger into the moistened puppy food and placing some on their lips. You'll be amazed at how quickly they can pick up on things, and they'll soon be lapping up the food quite eagerly. As the puppies' reliance on their mother's milk gradually lessens, you could also begin decreasing her regular diet, returning it to the normal amount of her food prior to pregnancy and lactation. This would allow her milk supply to gradually and naturally dry up.

The entire process will take time, even patience, from you. Just remember to keep the puppies and their living and feeding area clean, take care of the mother, socialize with the growing puppies as much as possible, and in no time, you'll have healthy puppies fully weaned and able to eat on their own.

Chapter Nine: Showing Your Toy Poodle

The important thing to remember is that dog shows are not a contest to determine which dog is better over all the others – it is a contest to determine which dog most closely adheres to the official and published breed standard. A good grounding on the prevailing breed standard for Toy Poodles is, therefore, important. On this point, please take note that for the AKC, the breed standards for Standard,

Miniature and Toy Poodles are the same except regarding height.

Below you will find a summary of the AKC Breed Standard for Toy Poodles. In this chapter, we also give you some guidelines, tips and tricks for preparing yourself and your dog for show. Joining a dog show can be a very rewarding and fun experience – not only will you learn a lot about your dog, the Toy Poodle breed, and yourself, it is also a chance to show off your beloved pet.

Always remember that the key to a good show is preparation and education. Make sure that you know what you are getting into – what is required of you and your dog, the rules and regulations, and what is involved in joining a dog show. And remember, too, to keep things light and fun, and just allow yourself to enjoy the experience.

Toy Poodle Breed Standard

General Appearance: Very active, intelligent and elegant appearance, squarely built and well-proportioned. Moves soundly and carries himself proudly. Properly clipped and carefully groomed, with an air of distinction and dignity.

Height: Toy Poodles are 10 inches or under at the highest point of the shoulders.

Temperament: Carries himself proudly, very active and intelligent, with an air of distinction and dignity peculiar to himself. Shyness or sharpness are considered major faults.

Head: Skull is moderately rounded, with a slight but definite stop. The cheekbones and muscles are flat.

Ears: Ears hang close to the head, set at or slightly below eye level. The ear leather is long, wide, and thickly feathered

Eyes: Eyes are dark and oval in shape, set far enough apart and positioned to create an alert and intelligent expression. Round, large or protruding eyes are considered major faults.

Muzzle: The muzzle is long, straight and fine, with a slight chiseling under the eyes. The lack of chin is considered a major fault.

Neck: The neck is well-proportioned, strong, and long enough to carry the head high and with dignity. The skin is snug at the throat.

Shoulders and Chest: Strong, smoothly muscled shoulders, with the shoulder blades well laid back and approximately the same length as the upper foreleg, a deep chest that is moderately wide with well sprung ribs.

Legs and Feet: Forequarters are straight and parallel when viewed from the front, strong pasterns, dewclaws may be removed. The feet are rather small, oval shaped with toes well arched and cushioned on thick firm pads. The feet turn neither in nor out.

Tail: The tail is straight, set high and carried up, docked of a sufficient length to ensure a balanced outline. Set low, curled, or carried over the back are considered major faults.

Coat Quality: Coat quality is of two kinds, either (1) Curly, of naturally harsh texture and dense throughout, or (2) Corded, hanging in tight, even cords of varying length.

Coat Colors: Only solid colored dogs, with acceptable varying shades of the same color, are acceptable in the AKC. Parti-colors, or dogs whose coats are two or more colors, are disqualified. Acceptable coat colors include blue, gray, silver, brown, café-au-lait, apricot, and cream, though varying shades may sometimes appear on the darker feathering of the ears and the tipping of the ruff. Such natural variation in the shading of the coat is not considered a fault.

Coat colors also determine the acceptable coloring of eyes and nose. Should the color of the nose, lips and eye rimes be incomplete, or the wrong color, it is considered a major fault.

- Brown and café-au lait Poodles have liver-colored noses, eye-rims and lips, dark toenails and dark amber eyes;
- Black, blue, gray, silver, cream and white Poodles have black noses, eye-rims and lips, black or self-colored toenails, and very dark eyes;

- The colors immediately preceding are also preferred for Apricots, though liver-colored noses, eye rims and lips, and amber eyes, are also permitted, though technically not desirable.

Coat Clips: The following are the acceptable coat clips. Take note that in all cases, shaping of the coat is permissible in order to ensure a neat appearance and a smooth, unbroken line. In all clips, the hair of the topknot may either be left free or held in place by elastic bands – this is the hair on the skull, from stop to occiput, and is the only area where elastic bands may be used. The hair should only be of sufficient length to present a smooth outline.

a. Puppy Clip – For poodles under 12 months. Any other Poodle 12 months or over must be shown in either the English Saddle or Continental Clip. Here, the coat is long, with the face, throat, feet and base of tail shaved. The entire shaven foot is visible, and there is a pompon on the end of the tail.

b. English Saddle Clip – Here, the face, throat, feet, forelegs and the base of the tail are shaved, with puffs on the forelegs and a pompon at the end of the tail. The hindquarters are covered with a short blanket of hair except for a curved saved area on each flank and two shaved bands on each hind leg. The entire shaven foot, as well as a portion of the shaven leg above the puff, are visible.

c. Continental Clip – The face, throat, feet, and base of the tail are shaved. The hindquarters are shaved, while pompons are optional on the hips. The legs are shaved, with bracelets on the hind legs and puffs on the forelegs. There is a pompon on the end of the tail, and the entire shaven foot and a portion of the shaven foreleg above the puff are visible.

d. Sporting Clip – For Stud and Brood Bitch classes, and in a non-competitive Parade of Champions, the Sporting Clip may be used. Hre, the face, feet, throat and base of tail are shaved, leaving a scissored cap on the top of the head and a pompon at the end of the tail. The rest are clipped or scissored to follow the outline of the dog, leaving a short blanket of coat no longer than one inch in length. The hair on the legs may be slightly longer than that on the body, however.

Preparing Your Toy Poodle for Show

Joining a dog show can be a very rewarding experience – not only do you get to mingle with other dog lovers and Toy Poodle aficionados, the period of preparation for a dog show will also teach you a lot about your own Toy Poodle and what it is that makes them so special.

Participation in a dog show is usually determined by registration – in the AKC, any dog that is 6 months or older and is included in a breed recognized by the club is eligible to join a dog show. Depending on where you live, the local kennel club nearest your area will usually have a similar requirement – as well as a published breed standard for Toy Poodles. Secure a copy of this breed standard early on – your period of preparation, which includes training, grooming, and care for your Toy Poodle will have you keeping one eye on the said breed standard.

The rules and regulations will also inform you about the possible disqualifications, faults, and other important information you will need to know – such as which particular show or category you are qualified to enter. Nothing can be more heartbreaking than to suffer a disqualification for not meeting a technical requirement you really should have known about early on. If you're feeling good about your chances, however, and your Toy Poodle just naturally seems to be meant for show, hunker down and prepare yourself and your dog for that fateful day.

It's also a good idea to attend one of these shows just to see what takes place – take note of which dogs are chosen as champions, what judges do when they judge each dog, and how dogs and owners comport themselves during a show. This is also a great time to network – ask questions, observe, make friends. You might even consider joining a match show in your area – these are fun, non-competitive shows that are a great place to practice and train both the dogs and novice exhibitors, and a great place for both to get their feet wet.

Once you deem yourself ready, check out the dog show calendars to determine when you feasibly join. This also gives you a date to shoot for as you begin to prepare yourself, and your dog, in earnest. Make inquiries, register well beforehand, and pay the required fees. Make sure that you have all the requisite documents ready to hand for the big day. Here are a few guidelines to keep in mind as you prepare for that show!

- Make sure that you're Toy Poodle is properly socialized.

Not only will you and your dog be spending the better part of a day in the company of a lot of other people and other dogs, you should also expect that your Toy Poodle will be handled by the judges. You don't want her growling or even showing timidity or shyness at this time – both of these are considered major faults. Neither would you want her to be barking continuously at all the strange people, dogs and things – it might give you a major headache, and would likely not rub off well on the judges, either. So make sure that your Toy Poodle is properly socialized, and that she is accustomed to being handled by strangers.

- Bathe, groom and clip beforehand

For Toy Poodles, especially, as with the other Poodle Types, only certain specific coat clips are acceptable. Long before the date of the dog show comes around, either you should have gotten adept at grooming and clipping your dog, or you have found a groomer you trust and rely on. Needless to say, preparing and grooming a Toy Poodle for show should not be done on the day itself – grooming a Poodle takes work, and you don't want to run out of time. How long does it usually take you to groom your Toy Poodle? Factor that in, as well as how long beforehand you can reasonably bathe her. Most owners give their dogs a bathe and a good grooming the day before the show itself, leaving plenty of time for the cut to set, but with plenty of time to spruce up the next day if needed. Judges will surely appreciate clean, neat-looking dogs in top condition.

- Take care of your dog's health.

A truly great show dog isn't made overnight – it can take months or years of care, training, and grooming to prepare your own dog. Regardless of how beautiful their clip is, or how intelligent your dog is, it will not matter much if your dog has the sniffles or is peculiarly weak or lethargic during the show. Judges will notice this. The quality of your dog's coat, in fact, the clearness of their eyes, their alertness and intelligence – all depends very much on just how healthy they are. Feed them well with nutritious food, give them plenty of mental and physical stimulation – take them out for walks and don't skimp on spending time with them for play. A happy, well-adjusted dog is, in itself, a beautiful sight to behold.

When the fateful day arrives, it is to be hoped that both you and your dog are fully prepared, well-rested, and ready to compete! Below are a final checklist of things to pack with you for the event. Other than these final items, take heart that you've done all you can to prepare, and regardless of whether or not your dog wins, the most important thing to remember at this point is to just enjoy the experience!

- Registration papers
- Water and a water bowl
- grooming kit
- show collar and leash
- trash bags
- any medication your dog may need
- toys to keep your dog amused and occupied
- snacks and treats
- paper towels

Chapter Ten: Keeping Your Toy Poodle Healthy

Toy Poodles can live a long, healthy and happy life – serving as your companion for years as long as you take care of them right. Feed them well, give them enough mental and physical stimulation, regular grooming and socialization – these are the bedrock for a pet who will live a long and happy life.

But as with most dogs, Toy Poodles as a breed can be prone to certain diseases or health conditions. In this chapter, we cover some of the more common health conditions that Toy Poodles can be prone to. Yes, there does seem to be a lot of them – that is why it is imperative that you purchase or acquire your Toy Poodle from a reputable breeder. Reputable breeders are those dedicated to perpetuating the best of the breed, and that does not only mean choosing breeding dogs for the ideal temperament, intelligence, or coat colors. It also means proper health screenings and avoiding the breeding of dogs with health conditions that they may pass on to their offspring.

It is important to remember, however, that even reputable breeders that do their best with their Toy Poodle lines will not be able to give you a 100% health guarantee. There is no such thing. Oftentimes, a health condition or sickness may just appear in one dog despite a breeder's best efforts. In these instances, the next best thing you can do is to arm yourself with education and information. Learn how to recognize the potential diseases that may afflict Toy Poodles, and with early detection, diagnosis and treatment, many of these illnesses can be managed well enough that they need not compromise your dog's health to any great degree.

Common Health Problems Affecting Toy Poodles

- Eye Conditions such as Progressive Retinal Atrophy (PRA), Cataracts, Glaucoma, Optic Nerve Hypoplasia, and Tear Staining
- Luxating Patella
- Legg-Calve-Perthes Disease

- Intervertebral Disk Disease (IVDD)
- Epilepsy
- Hypoglycemia
- Skin Tumors
- Tracheal Collapse
- Von Willebrand's Disease
- Addison's Disease
- Cushing's Disease
- Gastric Dilatation-Volvulus (Bloat)
- Sebaceous Adenitis

Eye Conditions

Poodles do suffer from a variety of eye problems and conditions – most of which are congenital or inherited. This is why it is a good idea to bring your Toy Poodle for an annual eye exam – even if he has already been certified as Clear, or even if the breeder has provided you with eye certifications for your dog's parents. The truth is, much is still unknown about congenital eye conditions in dogs, and some of the genes are recessive – which means that the gene can lie dormant in a line before suddenly showing up again in a distant offspring.

The good news is that the concerted efforts of dedicated Poodle breeders have made it easier to identify affected lines, and to remove them from breeding programs. While eye conditions in Toy Poodles has not precisely been eradicated, the incidence of it has certainly diminished because of the determination of these breeders.

Below are some of the more common eye conditions that affect Toy Poodles, their signs and symptoms, and the current state of available treatments of medications available.

Progressive Retinal Atrophy (PRA)

Toy Poodles are known to have a genetic predisposition to Progressive Retinal Atrophy (PRA), a condition which causes progressive blindness over time. The age of onset varies, but it typically appears during a dog's middle years, or from 3-8 years.

The initial symptoms may not be easy to spot at first – they can be very subtle, and because a dog will usually adjust and compensate for his increasing loss of vision, it may be some time before you become fully aware of the onset of this condition. Some of the first signs include dilated pupils, a characteristic shine to the eyes, or the loss of night vision – which can be seen from your dog's refusal to venture into a dark or dimly-lit room. Should cataracts also develop as a secondary condition, you might also notice what doctors call "cloudy eye." It must also be noted that PRA is not a painful condition unless there is complication resulting from a secondary condition, such as a inflammation.

Unfortunately, there is no effective treatment for PRA at this time. What an owner can do is to bring their Toy Poodle for an annual eye exam, and should your dog be diagnosed with PRA, he or she should no longer be bred from. It is interesting to note that the Poodle Club of America currently has an agreement with the Orthopedic Foundation for Animals (OFA) for the establishment of a database or Genetic Registry of the results of such eye screenings – and lists of whether a specific poodle is clear, a carrier, or affected with PRA. Clear or Carrier results require a $15 fee, while there is no charge for the inclusion of an Affected test result. This would certainly help hobbyists and breeders in the identification and selection of dogs who have been certified as clear of PRA for breeding.

If your Toy Poodle does develop PRA, a regular examination by a vet would keep down the chances of the development of secondary complications. Other than that, there are ways of helping them manage the condition. A blind dog should not be allowed outdoors, for instance, and their surroundings should be kept as familiar to them as possible in order to help them keep the capacity to navigate their environment.

Cataracts

Cataracts can be a congenital or inherited condition – and it seems that Poodles are among several canine breeds that are highly prone to congenital cataracts. It must be noted, however, that there are also other possible causes of cataracts – including diabetes, low calcium levels or hypocalcimia, malnutrition, eye injury, eye inflammation, or exposure to toxic substances or electric shock.

Cataracts cause a cloudiness in the lens of the eye, which opacity can be either partial or complete. Ideally, the lens should be clear – when it becomes cloudy, light cannot pass through to the retina, thus causing vision loss. Depending on the opacity of the lens, your Toy Poodle may only experience cloudy or blurred vision, or complete blindness. Cataracts are generally not painful, but if coupled with other conditions such as inflammation or fluid buildup and pressure within the eyeball, this can cause your dog pain and may eventually lead to permanent damage and irreversible vision loss.

The good news is that some forms of cataracts are removable by surgery. This largely depends, however, on your dog's condition and on whether surgery is advisable should there also be secondary conditions. Please consult your veterinarian as to the best course of treatment. Immediately after you observe a cloudiness in your dog's eyes, or if you notice a change in your dog's eye color to shades of gray, blue, or white, or if you notice an inflammation in or around the eye, seek medical attention to prevent the development of other complications. Immediate surgical treatment when feasible is always best so as to prevent the rapid development of the cataracts and its potentially irreversible progression into blindness.

Glaucoma

Another congenital condition affecting the eye to which Poodles are prone to is Glaucoma. This happens when there is inadequate fluid drainage in the eye, leading to the buildup of fluid and pressure on the eye. If the condition persists without treatment, it will eventually lead to permanent damage in the optic nerve, which will eventually lead to blindness.

Symptoms of glaucoma should be treated as an emergency – it is painful for one thing, and the lack of immediate treatment can lead to vision loss. If the condition persists for long without treatment, glaucoma affecting one eye can sometimes spread to the other eye.

Here are a few symptoms you should watch out for that may indicate the presence of pressure increase within the eye:

- Mild to severe pain in the eye, which can manifest through rubbing at the eye with a paw or on the floor)
- Redness of the eyes, or the distinct appearance of red vessels in the whites of the eye
- Cloudy cornea
- Squinting or tearing
- Light avoidance
- Pupil unresponsive to light

- Vision problems such as bumping into objects, unable to find things, or slow and careful walking
- A Bulging or swollen eye
- Fluttering eye lead
- The eyeball may recede back into the head
- Enlargement of the eyeball

In addition, this condition may also manifest through behavioral changes such as lack of appetite, anti-social behavior, or headaches that can be seen by the pressing of the head in order to relieve the pressure.

When your pet's glaucoma is caused by a genetic predisposition, this is known as Primary Glaucoma. If it is caused by external factors, on the other hand, such as infection, inflammation, injury or tumor, then this is known as Secondary Glaucoma.

The treatment of glaucoma depends on the symptoms and the severity of the condition. Either medication or surgery may be prescribed to help increase fluid drainage and/or to decrease fluid production) – mostly these are aimed to reducing pain and to slow the progression of he disease. If it is Secondary Glaucoma, then the underlying cause should be treated as well. A proper diagnosis is, therefore important in terms of providing the most appropriate treatment.

Even if the condition was caught early, you will still need to bring your dog back to your vet at least every six months in order to monitor the pressure within your dog's eyes. Long term, however, gradual vision loss for your dog is highly probable so you might want to discuss ways of managing your dog's condition with your vet.

Optic Nerve Hypoplasia

Optic Nerve Hypoplasia is, to put it simply, the underdevelopment of the optic nerve. This is a congenital condition, and quite rare, though some instances have been seen in certain breeds – including among Toy Poodles.

Optic Nerve Hypoplasia may affect one or both eyes, and the affected eye is frequently blind. But because one blind eye is often compensated for by the other, a unilateral affected eye can often go undetected. If affected, however, the pupil will show no responsiveness to light and is often excessively dilated. In certain instances, cataracts may also develop.

There is no cure or therapy for this condition, and prognosis is generally poor.

Tear Staining

Tear Staining may be considered the most common, and certainly the most visible of a Poodle's eye issues. This is recognizable by the red or rusty brown colored streaks that appear below the eyes – more prominently seen if your Toy Poodle has white or light-colored fur.

Tear Staining occurs due to excessive tear flow, or epiphora, which happens as a result of tear duct blockage or debris in the eyes. And while a dog's tears are clear, they also contain a pigment known as porphyrin, which is what causes streaking. Some of the other causes of tear staining include ingrown lashes, entropion (inverted eyelid), ear infection, medications, exposure to secondhand smoke, poor diet, plastic food bowls, stress, and even teething among puppies. The excessive tears are the eye's natural defense. In many cases, this is not a serious condition, and generally no more than an annoyance. Sometimes, however, it can be a sign of a more serious underlying health problem, such as when the tear stains result from glaucoma or another eye disease, eye infection, or a yeast infection. Bring your pet for a checkup in order to rule out possible health concern before attempting to address the staining.

In this instance, prevention of the condition from developing in the first place is key – by taking good care of your dog's eyes. Make face cleaning a regular part of his grooming ritual, and make sure that the hair near his eyes are trimmed. Other possible ways to prevent tear staining include feeding a high quality diet, giving him filtered drinking water instead of tap water, and using stainless steel bowls instead of plastic ones. And you can ask your vet to recommend a good and natural tearstain removal product.

Luxating Patella

A Luxating Patella occurs when the patella (knee cap) luxates or moves out or is pulled out of its normal position. When this happens, your dog may show a brief period of lameness that oddly enough seems to go away on its own. It can last for only a brief period, or sometimes longer such as several days, depending on the severity – after which he begins using his leg normally again as though nothing had happened.

If your Toy Poodle has a genetic predisposition to this condition, there is may be a malformation in the ridges of the patellar groove within which the patella moves. If the ridge is too shallow, for instance, a sudden movement may cause the patella to jump out of the groove, causing the leg to "lock up." The patella can only return to its normal position after the quadriceps muscles relax and increases in length, which is why it may take your dog some time to recover his normal walking posture. But while this may seem harmless and only manifesting in brief periods of lameness, it can also occur chronically – in which case the femur cartilage can gradually erode due to the constant stress and friction. Eventually, this may lead to osteoarthritis and occasionally, a ruptured cranial ligament.

Surgery can often be availed of as a treatment – where the groove at the base of the femur may be surgically deepened in order to better hold the kneecap in place.

Prognosis is usually good, and the dog can recover completely within the next 30-60 days. Surgery is not always necessary, however, and many dogs can still live long and healthy lives without developing pain or arthritis. Management of this condition includes supplements, minerals and vitamins, as well as recommended supportive exercises. Early diagnosis of this condition can help you manage your pet's condition earlier, and avoid the condition from worsening in the first place.

Legg-Calve-Perthes Disease (LCP)

Sometimes called Legg-Perthes Disease or Aseptic or Avascular Femoral Head and Neck Necrosis, this condition is more commonly seen among miniature, toy, and small-breed dogs, and involves a spontaneous degeneration or necrosis of the head on the femur bone in the hind leg(s). This usually shows from between 4-12 months of age, and more commonly affects only one hip.

The precise cause of this disease is still unknown, although the prevailing theory has to do with the blood supply to the head of the femur bone. Some of the symptoms include lameness, pain when moving the hip joint, and a gradual wasting of the muscles on the affected limb(s). X-rays can help diagnose the disease, by showing any changes in the bones and joints in the affected area.

Surgery to excise the affected femur bone head is the usual course of treatment – though painkillers and cold packs can with the lameness. Rehabilitation post-surgery will also be needed through periods of rest, regulated exercise and physical therapy. Swimming is a preferred course of treatment, as this can help develop the hind leg muscles while keeping your dog from bearing his weight on the affected legs.

Intervertebral Disk Disease (IVDD)

While the degeneration of the intervertebral disks in dogs occur naturally as they get older, sometimes this process occurs earlier, leading to what is called Intervertebral Disk Disease (IVDD).

When this happens, the jelly-like center of the disk becomes dehydrated due to loss of water, thereby resulting in the loss of its ability to absorb shock and to cushion the spine. As the degenerated disk is compressed, the force is then transferred to the outer rings of the disk, eventually causing tears. This can eventually lead to permanent nerve damage, so timely recognition of this condition and immediate intervention is important.

Watch out for the following symptoms as signs that something may be wrong:

- Neck pain and stiffness
- Back pain and stiffness
- Lowered head stance
- Abdominal tenderness or tenseness
- Arched back or hunched posture

- Incomplete urination
- Lameness or dragging one or more legs when walking
- Stiffness or weakness and a reluctance to rise
- Tremors, shaking, or trembling
- Lack of coordination and abnormal reflexes
- Collapsing or "knuckling over when walking or standing

These symptoms can manifest after acute physical trauma or after engaging in strenuous physical activities. It can sometimes be caused by some form of trauma such as injuries or other form of damage – and can even happen to healthy dogs. A predisposition is caused, however, by chondrodystrophy, or a cartilage formation disorder seen in angular limb deformities and abnormally short legs. Poodles are known as a chondrodystrophic breed.

Diagnosis is done by a neurologic examination by a Board-Certified veterinarian, and treatment can involve medication and/or surgery. Prognosis depends on the severity of the symptoms and the progress of the condition – often, the loss of sensation to the hind limbs is not a good sign. As long as there is some sensation left in the hindlimbs, some form of mobility may be recovered. The sooner surgery is performed, the greater the chances for recovery. This should be followed by post-surgical therapy and a controlled diet and exercise regimen.

Epilepsy

Idiopathic Epilepsy may affect all types of Poodles – whether Standard, Miniature, or Toy. Epilepsy is defined as having multiple seizures, while Idiopathic Epilepsy means that the cause is unknown. Idiopathic Epilepsy is also considered to be the most common seizure disorder among dogs.

External factors may cause seizures and epilepsy – factors such as lead poisoning, heat stroke, or any trauma to the head. Seizures may also be caused by brain damage, disease, or a tumor, or it may be the result of a genetic predisposition passed on by the dog's parents. In some instances, the cause may be metabolic – such as hypocalcemia, high blood ammonia levels, or hypoglycemia – the latter being a common cause among Toy Breed puppies.

The symptoms can vary, though they almost always consist of behaviors that owners find frightening: whining, shaking, nervousness, hiding, staggering, or acting frantic. They are often referred to by different terms such as convulsion, fit, epilepsy, or seizure, though they do generally mean the same thing. Sometimes the seizure is localized to a small area such as a limb or the face, but sometimes it can also spread throughout the body in a generalized convulsion. These can last from about 1-3 minutes, after which there is a post-ictal stage, or a period of disorientation until the dog comes out fully from his seizure. More often, this also involves a brief period of blindness. The post-ictal stage can last anywhere from less than an hour to two days. If your Toy Poodle is having a seizure, remain calm, and seek emergency care immediately. Needless to say, any dog that has been diagnosed with seizures or canine epilepsy should not be bred from, in case a predisposition is passed on to their offspring.

Diagnosis is of canine epilepsy is clinical, and made only after other possible causes are ruled out. Confirmation is made through various tests such as CT brain scans, EEG, MRI, spinal taps, and urine and blood testing. Other possible causes of seizure-like symptoms include cardiac and respiratory diseases or reverse sneezing.

Treatment depends on the cause and severity of the condition. If the seizures are the result of external factors, for instance, then the underlying condition or injury must also be treated. Treatment generally includes surgery and dietary changes, while anticonvulsant medication is used to treat and perhaps control the symptoms or the seizures. Epilepsy, however, is rarely cured or treated completely. With proper treatment, however, the frequency and severity of the seizures can be reduced to give the dog as normal and comfortable a life as possible.

Hypoglycemia

Puppies and toy breed dogs (even adult Toy breeds) such as the Toy Poodle are at risk from hypoglycemia. This is basically a condition where your dog can suffer from dangerously low blood sugar levels. Small dog breeds are particularly prone to this condition because of their low muscle mass, thus making the maintenance of proper glucose levels tougher. Low blood sugar levels can translate to low energy, and can be a potentially dangerous condition. Though hypoglycemia can vary from mild to moderate to severe, at the extreme, the brain can be affected and may sometimes lead to seizures.

The causes of hypoglycemia in dogs are varied, but may include any of the following:

- Inadequate meal spacing – or too long periods between meals, or skipping meals
- Addison's disease, which can reduce glucose formation or storage
- Too much exercise
- Lack of proteins in their diet
- Insulin overdose
- Abnormal hormone functions

Such conditions can also be exacerbated by stress, dietary changes, infections, poor nutrition, or low body temperatures. The symptoms of hypoglycemia, on the other hand, can range from any of the following:

- Lack of energy
- Weakness or lethargy
- Hunger
- Restlessness
- Shivering
- Disorientation
- Stupor
- Convulsions or seizures
- Head tilting
- Ataxia, or lack of muscle coordination
- Cold and white gums (instead of warm and pink)

As the owner, it is imperative that you are able to recognize and provide immediate relief to a dog suffering from hypoglycemia. Some of the recommended measures to address the symptoms of hypoglycemia include the immediate feeding of glucose sources such as ice cream, honey, sugar. These can be easily fed or administered to a dog in hypoglycemic shock – especially since a dog experiencing low sugar shock will generally not wish to eat or drink. You can use a syringe (without the needle) to feed honey to them, for instance, or use your finger to scrape some ice cream or honey at the back of their top front teeth. Repeat this as many times as necessary, until your dog begins to recover.

Most recommend that you always keep glucose sources ready in the fridge, or to bring them with you whenever you take your dog out for a walk, or go anywhere out of the house. This allows you to address any hypoglycemic symptoms immediately. Recovery can be as immediate as 10-20 minutes, or as long as several hours. Regardless, if your dog does not recover within 30 minutes, seek emergency services immediately.

Skin Tumors

You might occasionally encounter lumps on your dog's skin that just don't go away – these are skin tumors, and they can either be malignant or benign. Fortunately, many canine skin tumors are benign. These are usually just abnormal swellings in or beneath the skin, and may range in type from pimples, cysts, pustules, and the like.

It is always a good idea to have them checked by a vet for proper identification and diagnosis, however. A biopsy can help determine whether they are benign and non-threatening, or whether they require more intensive treatments. The recommended treatments will depend on what type of skin tumor it is. A malignant growth, for instance, that are often fast-growing and are prone to bleeding and ulceration, will require more aggressive treatments such as surgical removal, as opposed to a slow growing and harmless lump.

Tracheal Collapse

Tracheal Collapse happens when the trachea, or windpipe, literally collapses. This is a genetic condition which can be commonly seem among small and toy breeds such as the Toy Poodle, and takes place when the rings of cartilage which make up the tube that comprises the windpipe, begins to collapse.

This is another genetic condition, and is primarily ascribed to a congenital abnormality in which the tracheal rings are weaker than normal. The condition itself is exacerbated or brought on by other factors such as too much exercise, obesity, heat, eating, drinking, excitement or irritants such as dirt or smoke. As the tracheal rings begin to collapse, the following symptoms may appear:

- Labored breathing
- A characteristic honking cough
- A bluish tinge to the gums
- Unproductive vomiting
- Exercise intolerance
- Abnormally rapid breathing
- Spontaneous loss of consciousness

All of these symptoms can be traced to the narrowed air passageways and lack of oxygen. A definitive diagnosis of tracheal collapse is possible through a combination of radiographs, chest x-rays, bronchoscopy, and fluoroscopy.

Treatment mainly consists of cough suppressants, anti-inflammatories, and antibiotics. Weight loss is prescribed for dogs who are also suffering from obesity. Though not curative, prognosis is generally good after such treatments, with many dogs showing long term, positive response. In cases where such treatment does not result in a positive response, surgery may be availed of – though such surgical treatments are specialized and should only be performed by an expert.

If your dog is undergoing medical treatment for Tracheal Collapse, adherence to a strict lifestyle for your dog is essential to their recovery – weight management or weight loss, gentle exercise, avoiding stress and over-excitement, and a shift to a harness instead of a collar and leash is recommended.

Von Willebrand's Disease

Von Willebrand's Disease is a congenital bleeding disorder characterized by a deficiency of the von Willebrand Factor (vWF) – a necessary adhesive glycoprotein necessary for blood clotting. This is the most common hereditary bleeding disorder among dogs, and can lead to the lack or failure of clotting, and excessive bleeding after an injury.

Fortunately, a DNA test is now available to screen for the presence of the vWD gene, and responsible health screenings prior to breeding programs can hopefully prevent this disease from being passed on through generations.

The severity of the disease itself varies, and can range from very mild to very severe. Sometimes there will be spontaneous cases of bleeding such as nosebleeds or blood in the gums, urine, or feces. Other times, however, this condition only becomes noticeable after a trauma or injury wherein severe bleeding results. Should this happen, blood transfusion may be necessary.

Addison's Disease

Also known as hypoadrenocorticism, Addison's Disease is a condition whereby the adrenal glands do not produce sufficient hormones, such as mineralocorticoids and glucocorticoids. These hormones are necessary to the bodily functions, and deficient production can lead to the different kinds of symptoms which characterize Addison's Disease.

Some of these symptoms include:

- Lethargy
- Vomiting
- Weight loss
- Diarrhea
- Frequent urination
- Increased thirst
- Dehydration
- Weak pulse
- Low temperature
- Hair loss
- Painful abdomen
- Shaking
- Depression
- Collapse
- Blood in feces

Many of the initial symptoms that do appear are easily missed: vomiting, gastrointestinal disturbances, lethargy, and poor appetite. This condition has, in fact, been called the Great Imitator because of its similarity to other medical conditions. Diagnosis itself is not that easy, involving an analysis of your dog's medical history, a physical exam, and various lab tests such as blood count, biochemistry profile, and urinalysis. An ACTCH (adrenocorticotropic hormone) response test can confirm diagnosis – by the lack of response of the adrenal hormones. At present, there is no test that can identify carriers.

Treatment generally includes regular and long-term hormone treatments or supplements, though sometimes a severe or acute episode requires more immediate measures – including intravenous fluids. Quick action is necessary because an acute episode can be life-threatening. With regular treatment, however, the prognosis can be quite good, and many dogs can still go on to live a long, happy and healthy life.

Cushing's Disease

As opposed to the underproduction of adrenal hormones in Addison's Disease, Cushing's Disease is a condition characterized by the overproduction of cortisol by the adrenal glands. Some of the symptoms include eating more, drinking more, urinating more than usual, weight gain, hair loss, panting a lot, skin infections, and a swollen abdomen. These are signs that your dog may have Cushing's Disease.

Also known as hyperadrenocorticism, Cushing's Disease commonly appears among older dogs, and the symptoms are usually mistaken for the natural aging process. This can prompt some owners to consider putting their dogs to sleep, which is unfortunate because when properly diagnosed, Cushing's Disease is actually treatable.

Cortisol is what helps the body respond to stress, and affects a myriad of body functions such as blood sugar levels, metabolism, kidney function, the cardiovascular and nervous system, as well as a dog's immunity. When there is too much supply of cortisol in the body, it throws the body's feedback mechanism into whack, thus also compromising the body's ability to regulate these different functions.

Diagnosis is made from a combination of different tests. At first, depending on the findings of a blood and urine test where Cushing's Disease is probable, hormone screening tests may also be conducted, such as ACTCH Stimulation Test and a Low dose dexamethasone suppression (LDDS) test. An ultrasound can also tell your vet whether or not your dog has a tumor in the adrenal glands – which is one type of Cushing Disease that can affect dogs. The two other types are caused by a tumor in the pituitary gland, or as an effect of the long-term use of steroids and cortisone.

When possible, treatment can be done through a surgical removal of the tumor present. If it isn't caused by a tumor, or if removal of the tumor is not feasible, then medical treatments (or the control of in cause the cause is long-term steroid use) may be availed of. With proper management and treatment, your dog can still live a happy and healthy quality way of life.

Gastric Dilatation-Volvulus (Bloat and Torsion)

Bloat among dogs and Toy Poodles can be fatal. When there is too much gas or fluid in the dog's stomach, the stomach becomes distended. When this happens, the dog's stomach twists or rotates (thus, bloat and torsion). If the rotation is only partial, it is called gastric torsion. If the stomach rotates completely, however, it is called gastric volvulus. When this happens, there is no way for the gas to exit, and the blood supply is also cut off. This is extremely painful and constitutes a very real emergency. A dog with Gastric Dilatation-Volvulus will die if no immediate steps are taken.

It is not known why this happens among dogs, or why their stomach rotates. But some contributing factors may include eating large quantities of food, or exercising heavily within two hours of a meal. When you notice any of the following symptoms, it is possible that your Toy Poodle may be experiencing bloat:

- Extreme restlessness
- Vomiting, or attempting to vomit
- Pain in the abdomen
- Swollen stomach
- Rapid breathing
- Excessive salivation and drooling
- Pale gums

If you suspect that your dog is suffering from bloat, seek emergency medical services immediately. Ultimately, surgery may have to be performed.

Sebaceous Adenitis

This is an inflammatory skin disease that affects the sebaceous glands lining the hair follicles. These glands are gradually destroyed – and symptoms can range from dull and brittle hair to patchy areas of hair loss. Other possible symptoms include clumps of matted hair, intense itching and scratching, silver-white scales on the skin, or skin lesions that may form on areas of the head. Sometimes, secondary bacterial infection may develop along the hairline.

The condition is diagnosed through a skin biopsy, and treatment largely depends on the symptoms – shampoos, oils, supplements and other forms of medical treatment may be prescribed.

Preventing Illness with Vaccinations

There are many ways to ensure the continued good health of your Toy Poodle: be sure to purchase one from a reputable breeder that screens his breeding pair against some of the more common diseases that affect Poodles. Give your Toy Poodle sufficient exercise, mental stimulation, and a healthy and balanced diet, and your tiny dog can live for years. In fact, while the general lifespan of a Toy Poodle is about 15 years, some have been known to live for as long as 18-20 or more years. So take good care of your dog, and he will be a true lifelong companion.

One of the ways to ensure the continued good health of your pock is by having him vaccinated against some of the deadly illnesses that can afflict our canine friends. Many of these diseases have long been considered deadly to canines, but the development of the appropriate vaccines help your Toy Poodle develop an immunity against these diseases. They do this by the introduction of antigens that are similar to the disease (but not disease-causing) into your dog's system. This stimulates their immune system so that should they ever be exposed to the real thing, their immune system is prepared to recognize and fight off the said organisms.

In recent years, there has been a growing concern that perhaps too much vaccination may actually be harmful to your dog's health. It is important to note that while there may be some truth to this statement, what cannot be denied is that some form of vaccination is still necessary – particularly when it comes to the core vaccines. Perhaps the only variable is the question of when and how often to vaccinate.

Below we present you with a general vaccination schedule for Toy Poodles, but please take note that this is just a recommendation. The decision of when and how often to vaccinate your pet depends on you – and make sure it is a decision based on sufficient information. Ask your vet for his recommendations, and factor in your dog's weight, age, and any physical reaction he might show to any administered vaccine.

Vaccination Schedule for Toy Poodles **	
Age	Vaccine
5 weeks	Parvovirus
6-8 weeks	Adenovirus, Distemper, Hepatitis, Parainfluenza, Parvovirus
12 weeks	Rabies and Leptospirosis
14 weeks	Lyme Disease and Leptospirosis
16 weeks	Leptospirosis

** Keep in mind that vaccine requirements may vary from one region to another. Only your vet will be able to tell you which vaccines are most important for the region where you live.

Core vaccines are those which are recommended for all pets, while non-core vaccines are administered based only on the possible prevalence of the disease in your region, and your dog's risk of exposure.

Most dogs do not show any adverse reactions from vaccines, but should your dog begin showing any ill-effects that you think might be due to his vaccination, such as fever, vomiting, sluggishness, swelling, or loss of appetite, then bring him to a vet immediately.

Toy Poodle Care Sheet

1.) Basic Toy Poodle Information

Pedigree: Barbet, Hungarian Water Hound,

AKC Group: Toy Group

Types: In the AKC, the Toy Poodle is one variety of the Poodle Breed, along with Standard and Miniature Poodles. Size in the AKC is determined by height, not by weight.

Breed Size: small

Height: 10 inches (25.4 cm) or under at the highest point of the shoulders

Weight: 6-9 lbs (3-4 kg)

Coat Types: a single layer coat that is either dense and curly, or corded

Coat Texture: ranges from coarse and woolly to soft and wavy

Coat Clips: For conformation shows, acceptable clips in the AKC include the Puppy clip, English Saddle, Continental Clip, or Sporting Clip

Color: Solid colors or parti-colors ranging from blue, gray, silver, brown, apricot, café-au-lait, cream. Patterns include phantom, brindle and sable – but these are considered out of standard by all major registries.

Eyes: Eyes are dark and oval in shape

Ears: Hangs close to the head, with a thickly feathered and long ear leather

Tail: Straight, set high and carried up.

Temperament: Remarkably intelligent, highly responsive and very trainable. Sweet, cheerful, lively and perk, socializes well. Can sometimes be high strung or timid.

Strangers: Toy Poodles do well with people, though not recommended for the roughhousing play of children. They may have a tendency to bark a lot. They make great watchdogs.

Other Dogs: With proper socialization and enough exercise, Toy Poodles do well with other dogs.

Other Pets: With proper socialization and enough exercise, Toy Poodles do well with other pets

Training: Highly intelligent and very trainable

Exercise Needs: Toy Poodles are an active breed that need daily walks and regular play time.

Health Conditions: generally healthy but may be prone to certain health conditions such as Eye Conditions (Progressive Retinal Atrophy (PRA), Cataracts, Glaucoma, Optic Nerve Hypoplasia, and Tear Staining), Luxating Patella, Legg-Calve-Perthes Disease, Intervertebral Disk Disease (IVDD), Epilepsy, Hypoglycemia, Skin Tumors, Tracheal Collapse, Von Willebrand's Disease, Addison's Disease, Cushing's Disease, Gastric Dilatation-Volvulus (Bloat), and Sebaceous Adenitis

Lifespan: average 12-15 years or more

2.) Habitat Requirements

Recommended Accessories: dog bed, food/water dishes, toys, collar, leash, harness, grooming supplies

Collar and Harness: sized by weight

Grooming Supplies: bristle brush, hound glove with raised rubber nodes, or rubber curry

Grooming Frequency: Brush regularly or at least 2-3 times a week, with professional clipping at least every few weeks. Bathing can be done monthly or when he starts to get dirty or smelly.

Energy Level: high energy level; lack of exercise can lead to destructive behavior

Exercise Requirements: Low impact, moderate exercise such as regular walks of at least 60 minutes each day, and occasional games and play

Food/Water: stainless steel or ceramic bowls, clean daily

Toys: start with an assortment, see what the dog likes; include some mentally stimulating toys

3.) Nutritional Needs

Nutritional Needs: water, protein, carbohydrate, fats, vitamins, minerals

RER: 30(body weight in kilograms) + 70

Calorie Needs: higher calorie requirements per pound compared to larger breeds due to their fast metabolism, though calorie needs will still vary by age, weight, and activity level; RER modified with activity level

Amount to Feed (puppy): Free feeding is recommended for puppies

Amount to Feed (adult): consult recommendations on the package; calculated by weight. 3-5 well-spaced meals throughout the day is ideal to prevent hypoglycemic conditions

Important Ingredients: fresh animal protein (chicken, beef, lamb, turkey, eggs), digestible carbohydrates (rice, oats, barley), animal fats

Important Minerals: calcium, phosphorus, potassium, magnesium, iron, copper and manganese

Important Vitamins: Vitamin A, Vitamin A, Vitamin B-12, Vitamin D, Vitamin C

Look For: AAFCO statement of nutritional adequacy; protein at top of ingredients list; no artificial flavors, dyes, preservatives

4.) Breeding Information

Age of First Heat: Around 6 months old, sometimes earlier or later by a few months

Heat (Estrus) Cycle: 14 to 21 days

Frequency: twice a year, every 5 to 7 months

Greatest Fertility: 11 to 15 days into the cycle

Gestation Period: 59 to 63 days

Pregnancy Detection: possible after 21 days, best to wait 28-30 days before exam

Feeding Pregnant Dogs: maintain normal diet until week 4 or 5 then slightly increase rations by 20 to 50 percent for the last five weeks

Signs of Labor: body temperature drops below normal 100° to 102°F (37.7° to 38.8°C), may be as low as 98°F (36.6°C); dog begins nesting in a dark, quiet place

Contractions: period of 10 minutes in waves of 3 to 5 followed by a period of rest

Whelping: may last for about two to four hours or more, depending on the litter size

Puppies: born with eyes and ears closed; eyes open at 3 weeks, teeth develop at 10 weeks

Litter Size: average of 3 puppies

Size at Birth: about 6- 6 ½ oz.

Weaning: supplement with controlled portions of moistened puppy food at around 4 weeks, or when the mother starts losing interest in feeding the puppies. Fully weaned at 7-8 weeks

Socialization: start as early as possible to prevent puppies from being nervous as an adult, preferably before 14-16 weeks of age

Index

D

E

F

G

H

R

S

T

V

Photo Credits

Cover Page Photo By Dawn Huczek from USA via Wikimedia Commons. <https://commons.wikimedia.org/wiki/File:Did_you_call_me.jpg>

Page 1 Photo by Ojelle at the English language Wikipedia via Wikimedia Commons. <https://commons.wikimedia.org/wiki/File:Large_apricot_toy_poodle.jpg>

Page 9 Photo by Harpagornis via Wikimedia Commons. <https://commons.wikimedia.org/wiki/File:White_Toy_poodle.jpg>

Page 17 Photo by Pleple2000 via Wikimedia Commons. <https://commons.wikimedia.org/wiki/File:Pudel_toy_srebrny_67.jpg>

Page 25 Photo by V. Eickenberg via Wikimedia Commons. <https://commons.wikimedia.org/wiki/File:Pudel_Toyweiss.jpg>

Page 37 Photo by Kolbabka via Wikimedia Commons. <https://commons.wikimedia.org/wiki/File:Šmudla.JPG>

Page 43 Photo by Natox via Wikimedia Commons. <https://commons.wikimedia.org/wiki/File:ToyPoodlePup.jpg>

Page 51 Photo by Yasuhiko Ito from Sendai, Japan via Wikimedia Commons. <https://commons.wikimedia.org/wiki/File:Toy_Poodle_ Chocolat_(3128772945).jpg>

Page 61 Photo by mschiffm via Pixabay. <https://pixabay.com/en/dog-toy-poodle-pet-animal- 706958/>

Page 69 Photo by Sanna Vilma Kristiina Vitikainen via Wikimedia Commons. <https://commons.wikimedia.org/wiki/File:Toy_%27parti %27_poodle_puppies_-_1.JPG>

Page 81 Photo by Томасина via Wikimedia Commons. <https://commons.wikimedia.org/wiki/File:Toy_Poodle_i n_Riga_3.JPG>

Page 91 Photo by Manuel Gonzalez Olaechea y Franco via Wikimedia Commons. <https://commons.wikimedia.org/wiki/File:CanichesToy.J PG>

Page 121 Photo by Colliluca at Italian Wikimedia via Wikimedia Commons. <https://commons.wikimedia.org/wiki/File:Gently_Born_ Papriche_5.jpg>

References

"Addison's Disease in Dogs." PetMD.
<http://www.petmd.com/dog/conditions/endocrine/c_dg
_hypoadrenocorticism>

"American Kennel Club Official Standard of the Poodle."
AKC.
<http://images.akc.org/pdf/breeds/standards/Poodle.pdf?
_ga=1.209273170.114591122.1478283632>

"All About Toy Poodles." Pet360.
<http://www.pet360.com/dog/breeds/all-about-toy-
poodles/rR6ys7c-q0-qLOWsclGW_g>

"Ask a Vet: Are the Small Lumps On My Dog's Skin
Serious?" Washingtonian Staff.
<https://www.washingtonian.com/2014/12/10/ask-a-vet-
are-the-lumps-on-my-dog-serious/>

"Best Dog Food for Toy Poodles: Feeding the Play Machine."
HerePup. <http://herepup.com/best-dog-food-for-toy-
poodles/>

"Bleeding Disorder in Dogs." PetMD.
<http://www.petmd.com/dog/conditions/cardiovascular/
c_dg_von_willebrand_disease>>

"Canine Cushing's Disease." Kate Connick © 2002.
<http://www.kateconnick.com/library/cushingsdisease.ht
ml>

"Cataracts in Dogs." PetMD.
<http://www.petmd.com/dog/conditions/eye/c_dg_catara
ct#>

"Cataracts in Poodles." Nicholas Cassotis, DVM, DACVO.
<http://www.ivghospitals.com/specialty-
services/cataracts-in-poodles/>

"Collapse of the Wind Pipe in Dogs." PetMD.
<http://www.petmd.com/dog/conditions/respiratory/c_d
g_tracheal_collapse>

"Crate Training." American Dog Trainers Network.
<http://inch.com/~dogs/cratetraining.html>

"Cushing's Syndrome in Dogs." WebMD.
<http://pets.webmd.com/dogs/cushings-syndrome-dogs>

"Detecting Addison's Disease in Your Dog." CJ Puotinen
and Mary Straus. <http://www.whole-dog-
journal.com/issues/14_10/features/Detecting-Addisons-
Disease-in-Your-Dog_20365-1.html>

"Dog Behavior Training – Proven Techniques to Help Solve
Problem Behaviors. Dog Training Central.
<http://www.dog-obedience-training-review.com/dog-
behavior-training.html>

"Dog Nutrition Tips." ASPCA. <http://www.aspca.org/pet-care/dog-care/dog-nutrition-tips>

"Epilepsy in a Poodle." Francine Richards. <http://pets.thenest.com/epilepsy-poodle-6105.html>

"Estrus Cycle in Dogs." VCA. <http://www.vcahospitals.com/main/pet-health-information/article/animal-health/estrus-cycles-in-dogs/5778>

"Feeding a Poodle." All Poodle Info. <http://www.allpoodleinfo.com/poodle-feeding>

"Feeding Dogs: Guide to the Small Dog Diet." Small Dog Place. <http://www.smalldogplace.com/feeding-dogs.html>

"General Poodle Information." The Pampered Poodle Palace. <http://www.thepamperedpoodlepalace.com/cratetrainingcare.htm>

"Genetic Cataracts in Poodles." Brandy Burgess. <http://pets.thenest.com/genetic-cataracts-poodles-9309.html>

"Genetic Welfare Problems of Companion Animals." UFAW. <http://www.ufaw.org.uk/dogs/poodle---hereditary-cataract>

"Getting Started Showing Your Dog." AKC.
<http://www.akc.org/events/conformation-dog-shows/getting-started-showing/>

"Glaucoma in Dogs." PetMD.
<http://www.petmd.com/dog/conditions/eyes/c_dg_glaucoma>

"Glaucoma in Dogs." Vetary.com.
<https://www.vetary.com/dog/condition/glaucoma>

"Grooming the Poodle." Cathy McGinnis.
<http://www.thedogplace.org/BREEDS/Poodle/Grooming_McGinnis.asp>

"Grooming Tips for Adult Toy Poodles." Jane Williams.
<http://pets.thenest.com/grooming-tips-adult-toy-poodles-8388.html>

"Health Issues in Poodles." The Poodle Club of America.
<http://www.poodleclubofamerica.org/all-about-poodles/health-concerns#bloat>

"Health Testing in Poodles." PCA.
<http://www.poodleclubofamerica.org/files/Health_Testing_in_Poodles.pdf>

"Housebreaking (Potty Training) for Puppies and Adult Dogs." Michele Welton.
<http://www.yourpurebredpuppy.com/training/articles/dog-housebreaking.html>

"Housebreaking Your Poodle Puppy." Rox. <http://www.luvmypoodle.com/housebreaking-your-poodle-puppy/#.WCi4MZc2vIU>

"How to Break 7 Common Bad Dog Habits." Shayna Meliker. VetStreet. <http://www.vetstreet.com/our-pet-experts/how-to-break-7-common-bad-dog-habits>

"How to Choose a Good Puppy (Picking the Best Puppy in a Litter)." Michele Welton. <http://www.yourpurebredpuppy.com/buying/articles/how-to-choose-a-puppy.html>

"How to Choose an Experienced Dog Breeder." PetMD. <http://www.petmd.com/dog/care/evr_dg_breeders>

"How to Choose High-Quality Dog Food." Alphadog. <https://alphadogfood.com/choose-high-quality-dog-food>

"How to Find a Responsible Dog Breeder." The Humane Society of the United States. <http://www.humanesociety.org/issues/puppy_mills/tips/finding_responsible_dog_breeder.html?referrer=https://www.google.com/>

"How to Groom a Poodle." Kelly Roper. <http://dogs.lovetoknow.com/wiki/How_to_Groom_a_Poodle>

"How to Prevent Tear Stains on Your Dog's Face." AKC. <http://www.akc.org/content/dog-care/articles/tear-stains/>

"Hypoglycemia – Low Blood Sugar." Douglas Brum, DVM. <http://www.canine-epilepsy-guardian-angels.com/hypoglycemia.htm>

"Hypoglycemia Requires Quick Intervention in Toy Breeds." Purina Pro Club. <https://purinaproclub.com/resource-library/pro-club-updates/hypoglycemia-requires-quick-intervention-in-toy-breeds/>

"Inflammatory Skin Disease in Dogs." PetMD. <http://www.petmd.com/dog/conditions/skin/c_dg_seba ceous_adenitis>

"Intervertebral Disk Disease (IVDD)." ExpertVet. <http://www.expertvet.com/articles/intervertebral-disk-disease-ivdd>

"Is a Poodle Right for Me?" Coastal Poodle Rescue. <http://www.coastalpoodlerescue.org/more-information/is-a-poodle-for-me>

"Keeping Your Puppy Safe at Home." Erin Ollila. <http://www.hillspet.com/en/us/dog-care/new-pet-parent/puppy-proofing-your-home>

"Knee Problems In Your Dog: Patellar Luxation – Luxating Kneecaps." 2ndchance.info./Ronald Hines. <http://www.2ndchance.info/patella.htm>

"Legg-Calve-Perthes disease." UPEI.
<http://discoveryspace.upei.ca/cidd/disorder/legg-calvé-perthes-disease>

"Legg-Calve-Perthes Disease in Dogs." PetMD.
<http://www.petmd.com/dog/conditions/musculoskeletal/c_dg_legg_calve_perthes_disease>

"Look Out: The Skinny on Poodle Eye Problems." Laura Harris. <http://herepup.com/look-skinny-poodle-eye-problems/>

"Luxating Patella." Race Foster, DVM.
<http://www.peteducation.com/article.cfm?c=2+2084&aid=457>

"New to Dog Showing?" The Kennel Club.
<http://www.thekennelclub.org.uk/activities/dog-showing/new-to-dog-showing/>

"Nutritional Differences for Small, Toy, and Large Breed Dogs." PetMD.
<http://www.petmd.com/blogs/nutritionnuggets/jcoates/2012/feb/nutrition_differences_for_small_toy_large_breeds-12459>

"Optic Nerve Hypoplasia." Go Pets America.
<http://www.gopetsamerica.com/dog-health/optic-nerve-hypoplasia.aspx>

"Optic Nerve Hypoplasia." Vetbook.org.
<http://www.vetbook.org/wiki/dog/index.php?title=Optic_nerve_hypoplasia>

"Owning a Dog Cost." Costhelper.
<http://pets.costhelper.com/owning-dog.html>

"People Foods to Avoid Feeding Your Pets." ASPCA.
<http://www.aspca.org/pet-care/animal-poison-control/people-foods-avoid-feeding-your-pets>

"Poodle." Wikipedia.
<https://en.wikipedia.org/wiki/Poodle#Coat>

"Poodle." AKC. <http://www.akc.org/dog-breeds/poodle/>

"Poodle Behavior." All Poodle Info.
<http://www.allpoodleinfo.com/poodle-behavior>

"Poodle Breeding." All Poodle Info.
<http://www.allpoodleinfo.com/breeding-poodles>

"Poodle Care and Tips." Grooming Angel Pet Salon.
<http://www.groomingangel.com/id64.html>

"Poodle Coat & Hair Issues." All Poodle Info.
<http://www.allpoodleinfo.com/poodle-coat-hair>

"Poodle Exercise Requirements." All Poodle Info.
<http://www.allpoodleinfo.com/poodle-exercise>

"Poodle Grooming Tools." All Poodle Info.
<http://www.allpoodleinfo.com/poodle-grooming-tools>

"Poodle Health Concerns." Allpoodleinfo.com. <http://www.allpoodleinfo.com/poodle-health-problems>

"Poodle Heat." All Poodle Info. <http://www.allpoodleinfo.com/poodle-heat-cycle>

"Poodle Training & Poodle Breed Information." Complete Guide to Responsible Dog Ownership. <http://www.dog-obedience-training-review.com/poodle-training.html#poodle training>

"Poodle Weight Chart." Tea Cup Poodles. <http://www.teacuppoodles.us/poodle_sizes1.htm>

"Poodles & Eye Diseases." Quentin Coleman. <http://pets.thenest.com/poodles-eye-diseases-4954.html>

"Potty Training Your Standard Poodle." The Pampered Poodle Palace. <http://www.thepamperedpoodlepalace.com/pottytraining101.htm>

"prcd-PRA Test" Optigen. <http://www.optigen.com/opt9_test_pra_poodle.html>

"Preparing for a dog show." Your Dog. <http://www.yourdog.co.uk/Dog-Activities/preparing-for-a-dog-show.html>

"Progressive Retinal Atrophy – toy, miniature (and standard) Poodles – Poodle." Orivet.

<http://orivet.com.au/progressive-retinal-atrophy-toy-miniature-and-standard-poodles-poodle/>

"Progressive Retinal Atrophy (PRA)." Davies Veterinary Specialists. <http://vetspecialists.co.uk/factsheets/Ophthalmology_Facts/Progressive_Retinal_Atrophy.html>

"Puppy proofing basics." Wendy Wilson. <https://www.cesarsway.com/dog-care/puppies/puppy-proofing-basics>

"Registered Standard Poodles with Addison's Disease (Hypoadrenocorticism)." Poodle Health Registry. <http://www.poodlehealthregistry.org/docs/Standard/PHR_Standard_Addison.html>

"Responsible Breeding." AKC. <http://www.akc.org/dog-breeders/responsible-breeding/>

"Rewards Based Dog Training – Without Using Treats!" Whole Dog Journal. <http://www.whole-dog-journal.com/issues/14_7/features/Reward-Based-Training-Without-Treats_20304-1.html>

"Routine Vaccinations for Puppies and Dogs." WebMD. <http://pets.webmd.com/dogs/guide/routine-vaccinations-puppies-dogs>

"Sebaceous Adenitis – standard (and toy) Poodle – Poodle." Orivet. <http://orivet.com.au/sebaceous-adenitis-standard-and-toy-poodle-poodle/>

"Seizures in Dogs." Thomas K. Graves, DVM.
    <http://www.canine-epilepsy.com/Graves.html>

"Skin Tumors in Dogs (Benign & Malignant)." PetWave.
    <http://www.petwave.com/Dogs/Health/Skin-
    Tumors.aspx>

"Sleeping Arrangement for New Puppy." BFF Dog Training
    LLC. <http://www.bfftraining.com/available-
    puppies/puppy-behavior-problems/sleeping-
    arrangement-for-new-puppy/>

"Socializing Your Dog." Le poodles guide. <http://www.le-
    poodles-guide.com/socializing-your-dog.html>

"Socializing Your Puppy or Adult Dog To Get Along With
    The World." Michele Welton.
    <http://www.yourpurebredpuppy.com/training/articles/
    dog-socializing.html>

"Symptoms of Intervertebral Disc Disease in Dogs."
    PetWave.
    <http://www.petwave.com/Dogs/Health/Intervertebral-
    Disk-Disease/Symptoms.aspx>

"Ten Tips for Showing Your Dog." Kelly Roper.
    <http://dogs.lovetoknow.com/dog-information/ten-tips-
    showing-your-dog>

"The Dangers of Hypoglycemia in Small Dogs and How to
    Prevent It." Swank Pets Dog Blog.

<http://www.swankpets.com/blog/2007/08/the-dangers-of-hypoglycemia-in-small-dogs-and-how-to-prevent-it/>

"The Evolution of the Toy Poodle." Pedigree. <http://www.pedigree.com/All-Things-Dog/Article-Library/The-Evolution-Of-The-Toy-Poodle.aspx>

"The Healthiest Foods for Toy Poodles." Sarah Whitman. <http://pets.thenest.com/healthiest-foods-toy-poodles-10829.html>

"The Hidden Message Behind Your Pet's Tear Stains." Dr. Karen Becker. <http://healthypets.mercola.com/sites/healthypets/archive/2014/11/12/pet-tear-staining.aspx>

"The Stages of Puppy Growth." Josh Weiss-Roessler. <https://www.cesarsway.com/dog-behavior/puppies/the-stages-of-puppy-growth-and-development>

"The Toy Poodle's 5 Biggest Health Risks." Pedigree. <http://www.pedigree.com/All-Things-Dog/Article-Library/The-Toy-Poodle-s-5-Biggest-Health-Risks.aspx>

"Thinking of Buying a Puppy? Find a Responsible Breeder." AKC. <http://www.akc.org/press-center/facts-stats/responsible-breeders/>

"Tips for Choosing a Healthy Puppy." Susan Koranki. <http://www.fidosavvy.com/choosing-a-healthy-puppy.html>

"Toy Poodle." Dog Breed Info Center.
<http://www.dogbreedinfo.com/toypoodle.htm>

"Toy Poodle." PetMD.
<http://www.petmd.com/dog/breeds/c_dg_toy_poodle>

"Toy Poodle." VetStreet.
<http://www.vetstreet.com/dogs/toy-poodle>

"Toy Poodle FAQ: Frequently Asked Questions About Toy Poodle Dogs." Michele Welton.
<http://www.yourpurebredpuppy.com/faq/toypoodles.html>

"Toy Poodle Health Problems and Raising a Toy Poodle Puppy to be Healthy." Michele Welton.
<http://www.yourpurebredpuppy.com/health/toypoodles.html>

"Toy Poodle Information." Next Day Pets.
<http://www.nextdaypets.com/Poodle-Toy.htm>

"Toy Poodle: The Right Breed For You?" Small Dog Place.
<http://www.smalldogplace.com/toy-poodle.html>

"Toy Poodle Temperament What's Good About 'Em, What's Bad About 'Em." Michele Welton.
<http://www.yourpurebredpuppy.com/reviews/toypoodles.html>

"Toy Poodles & It's Exercise Needs." Train Pet Dog.
<http://www.trainpetdog.com/toy-poodle_articles.html>

"Toy Poodles: What a Unique Breed!" AAMC.
   <http://aubreyamc.com/canine/toy-poodle/>

"Tracheal Collapse in Dogs." WebMD.
   <http://pets.webmd.com/dogs/tracheal-collapse-dogs>

"Treatment Options For Your Dog's Luxating Patella." Dr.
   Julie Mayer.
   <http://www.dogsnaturallymagazine.com/treatment-
   options-for-the-luxating-patella/>

"Understanding Bloat and Torsion." Kifka Borzoi.
   <http://www.kifka.com/Elektrik/Bloat.htm>

"Vaccinations For Your Pet." ASPCA.
   <http://www.aspca.org/pet-care/general-pet-
   care/vaccinations-your-pet>

"Vaccination Schedule for Dogs and Puppies."
   PetEducation.
   <http://www.peteducation.com/article.cfm?c=2+2115&aid
   =950>

"Vaccinating Your Pet." RSPCA.
   <https://www.rspca.org.uk/adviceandwelfare/pets/gener
   al/vaccinating>

"Want to Do Well at the Dog Show? Prepare All You Can
   Ahead of Time." AKC.
   <http://www.akc.org/content/dog-
   training/articles/prepare-ahead-of-time/>

"Weaning Puppies." Race Foster, DVM.
<http://www.peteducation.com/article.cfm?c=2+1651&aid
=887>

"Weaning Puppies from their Mother." PetMD.
<http://www.petmd.com/dog/puppycenter/nutrition/evr
_dg_weaning_puppies_from_their_mother#>

"Weaning Puppies: What to Do." WebMD.
<http://pets.webmd.com/dogs/weaning-puppies-what-
do>

"What to Do Quickly if Your Pet Stars Limping." Dr. Karen
Becker.
<http://healthypets.mercola.com/sites/healthypets/archiv
e/2015/01/04/legg-calve-perthes-disease.aspx>

"What You Need to Know About Collapsing Tracheas in
Dogs." Dr. Donna Spector, DVM, DACVIM.
<http://www.vetstreet.com/our-pet-experts/what-you-
need-to-know-about-collapsing-tracheas-in-dogs>

"Where Should My Puppy Sleep?" Katarina.
<http://doglifetraining.com/2012/08/where-should-my-
puppy-sleep/>

Feeding Baby
Cynthia Cherry
978-1941070000

Axolotl
Lolly Brown
978-0989658430

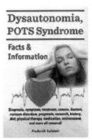

Dysautonomia, POTS
Syndrome
Frederick Earlstein
978-0989658485

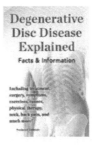

Degenerative Disc
Disease Explained
Frederick Earlstein
978-0989658485

Sinusitis, Hay Fever,
Allergic Rhinitis Explained
Frederick Earlstein
978-1941070024

Wicca
Riley Star
978-1941070130

Zombie Apocalypse
Rex Cutty
978-1941070154

Capybara
Lolly Brown
978-1941070062

Eels As Pets
Lolly Brown
978-1941070167

Scabies and Lice Explained
Frederick Earlstein
978-1941070017

Saltwater Fish As Pets
Lolly Brown
978-0989658461

Torticollis Explained
Frederick Earlstein
978-1941070055

Kennel Cough
Lolly Brown
978-0989658409

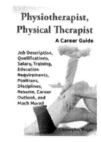

Physiotherapist, Physical
Therapist
Christopher Wright
978-0989658492

Rats, Mice, and Dormice
As Pets
Lolly Brown
978-1941070079

Wallaby and Wallaroo Care
Lolly Brown
978-1941070031

Bodybuilding Supplements
Explained
Jon Shelton
978-1941070239

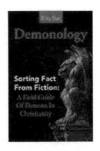

Demonology
Riley Star
978-19401070314

Pigeon Racing
Lolly Brown
978-1941070307

Dwarf Hamster
Lolly Brown
978-1941070390

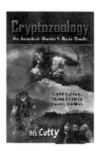

Cryptozoology
Rex Cutty
978-1941070406

Eye Strain
Frederick Earlstein
978-1941070369

Inez The Miniature Elephant
Asher Ray
978-1941070353

Vampire Apocalypse
Rex Cutty
978-1941070321

75714759R00095

Made in the USA
Middletown, DE
07 June 2018